Ronny Bar
Profiles

British Two-Seaters
of the Great War

Dedicated to Martiña...

CONTENTS

FOREWORD

I first became aware of Ronny Bar when a feature on the giant Handley-Page V/1500 bomber I had published in 2006, in Vol. 22, No. 5, of the late, lamented, Windsock magazine appeared with his colour views of the bomber. The work was so detailed that the small internal pages did not do it justice and the editor, Ray Rimell, published large views on the cover that showed the crew's leather seats and fully rendered floor boards.

The following year my wife and I were guests of Peter Jackson at the Classic Fighters airshow at Blenheim in New Zealand's South Island. At the dinner that Peter gave to bring those that had contributed to the show I saw the name Ronny Bar and went and asked if he was "THE" Ronny Bar..!

Since that time, Ronny and I have worked together on and off, mainly on Windsock Datafiles. Ronny's years of studying World War I aircraft is shown in his detailed profiles. He has been the profile artist who has brought to life the Wingnut Wings series of model aircraft construction kits. I am always astonished at his skill in interpreting faded black and white photographs and bring the aircraft to life in two dimensions.

This book covers the British two-seater aircraft of the war. With all the focus on the fighter aces it is not recognized these days that the two-seaters won World War I. The war was a modern artillery war and the work of the two-seaters on battery and counter-battery work, reconnaissance, and bombing dominated the sky. The fighter aircraft was developed to attack and deny the enemy two-seaters the opportunity for such work. Fighter versus fighter conflicts occurred as each side strove to achieve aerial supremacy so that their two-seaters could operate unmolested.

It is a pleasure to see Ronny's work presented in this format which offers a large enough easel to show his meticulous work and where the colours of these remarkable World War I aeroplanes can be realized and enjoyed.

Colin Owers

PREFACE

Dreams are there for chasing! And this book has been quite a long cherished dream for me.

Indeed, the idea of this book hasn't come out of the blue; the thought of gathering my profiles together has been in my head for quite some time. However, the biggest boost was that over the years I have been greatly and regularly encouraged to publish a book with my profile artwork by dozens of enthusiasts, modelers and readers all around the world, to whom I will always be grateful.

Once the idea took shape in my mind though, it was quite difficult to find enough free time within my fortunately tight schedule of commissioned profile jobs to devote to the task as it deserved... So, obviously this has been a rather slow process.

Anyway, after so many years illustrating books and articles by so many famed and admired writers in the Aviation field, finally here it is: MY OWN BOOK!

When I was a boy and was going to buy a book or a magazine, the first thing I looked for was whether it included profiles or not, and there I realized how important these are in every book about the History of Aviation, and above all, how necessary are these for us modelers.

At first I thought about writing some kind of text, but very quickly I realized that whatever I could say about these airplanes has already been written in countless books and articles by people much more versed than me on this subject, and that my field of action and what readers would really want when buying this book would be the profiles, so I decided to base this book only on these, with a minimum of data on each subject.

The spectrum of aircraft types that served during the Great War is so wide that it would be impossible to cover everything in a single volume, so it was necessary to divide it into categories. The first of these that came to my mind was that of the British two-seaters, a topic that personally, is one of my favorites.

The two-seater airplanes were the workhorses of a fledgling new weapon, the tools of everyday work over the trenches. They were without the glamour of the media, such as the fighter pilots enjoyed, but they were the seeds for the birth of a new age in warfare: the Age of Air Power!

It can't be said that those machines built in the United Kingdom were particularly aesthetically appealing, but their purposeful look, with such a practical approach to mechanical matters, makes them pretty attractive for an enthusiast like me.

Even more after having had the chance, invited by Sir Peter Jackson, to fly as an observer on the FE2b and the BE2e of The Vintage Aviator Ltd collection at the Hood aerodrome, in Masterton, New Zealand, in April 2009... What an experience!

Got to really admire those guys that went to war in those amazing machines… And with no parachutes!

At no time have I tried to cover all the two-seaters designed and built in Great Britain during the war; I have only selected those that, in my humble opinion, are the most important and most iconic.

Some of these profiles have been previously published by Albatros Publications and Wingnut Wings, but most were done especially for this book.

All profiles have been based on photographic evidence. Each subject was thoroughly researched, and although in some cases I have had no choice but to resort to empirical knowledge, "If a raven is black, all ravens are black" (Alan Toelle's dixit), I tried to be as accurate as it is possible to be with facts from more than 100 years ago. I have always kept in my mind what my dear friend Juanita Franzi once told me: "We're not just illustrators, we are visual historians!"

Ronny Bar

ACKNOWLEDGMENTS

I'll be forever grateful to Sir Peter Jackson, to whom I'll be in debt for several lifetimes!

To Richard Alexander, for the support and patience during all this time working together in the amazing Wingnut Wings, and for the friendship we built during my times in New Zealand.

To Ray Rimell, for his enduring trust in my work and his generous support throughout all these years.

To Ray again, and also to Colin Huston, Jack Herris, Aaron Weaver, and other publishers: For publishing my work and making it known by thousands of readers and enthusiasts all around the world.

To authors and writers Colin Owers, Greg VanWyngarden, Peter Kilduff, Alan Toelle, Josef Scott, Jim Wilberg, Bruno Schmaeling, Gregory Alegi, Paolo Varriale, Paul Hare, JS Alcorn, Mark Wilkins, Xavier Chevallier: for trusting me to illustrate their wonderful books and articles and for sharing their huge knowledge and expertise to help me improve my work.

To Eugene Ushakow, who whenever I asked provided me with invaluable information.

To my colleague artists: Juanita Franzi, Russell Smith, Robert Karr, Bob Pearson, Jim Miller, Dave Douglas, Steve Anderson, Mark Miller, Tomasz Gronczewski, Piotr Mrozoswski, Jerry Boucher: For their exquisite and always inspiring artwork, and for the good vibes I've always received from them.

To my friend Claudio Meunier: For his invaluable advice and help in the layout of this book and for the joy of his friendship.

And to my friends and comrades: Hector Martin Afllitto Echagüe and Diego Fernetti: For encouraging and supporting me to enter this fascinating world of professional aircraft profiling.

R.A.F. BE2a

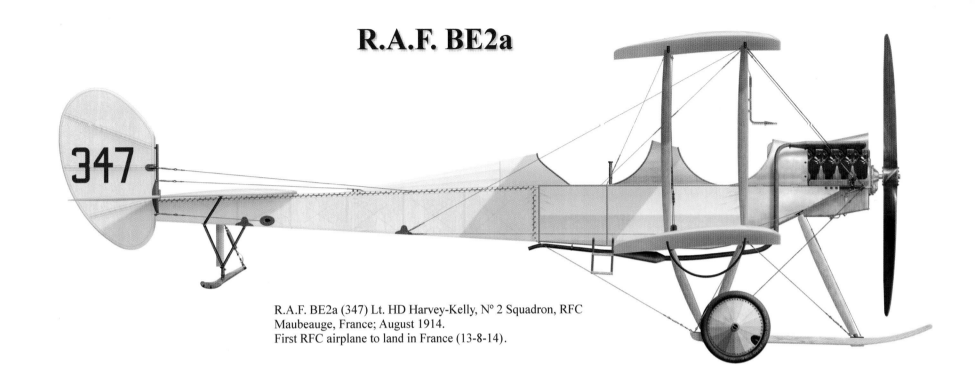

R.A.F. BE2a (347) Lt. HD Harvey-Kelly, Nº 2 Squadron, RFC
Maubeauge, France; August 1914.
First RFC airplane to land in France (13-8-14).

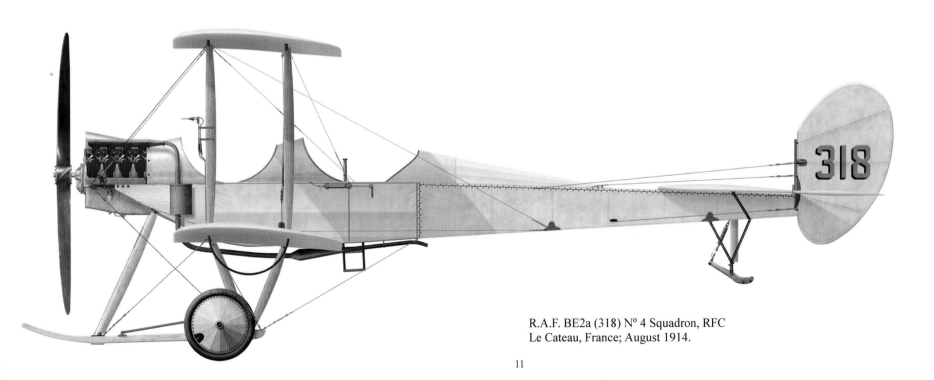

R.A.F. BE2a (318) Nº 4 Squadron, RFC
Le Cateau, France; August 1914.

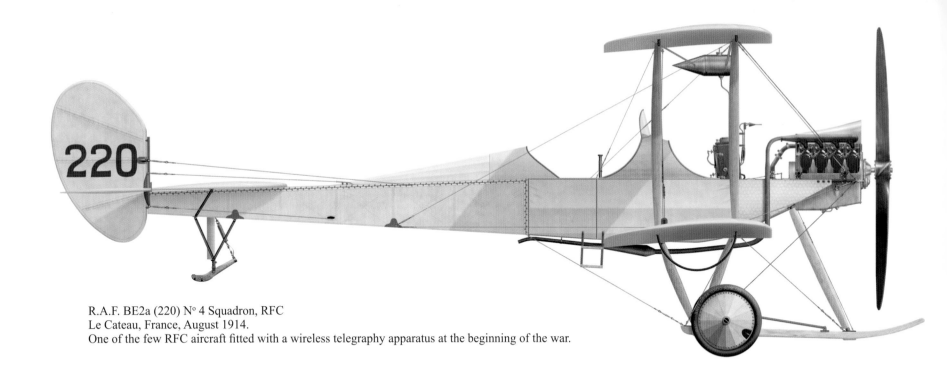

R.A.F. BE2a (220) Nᵒ 4 Squadron, RFC
Le Cateau, France, August 1914.
One of the few RFC aircraft fitted with a wireless telegraphy apparatus at the beginning of the war.

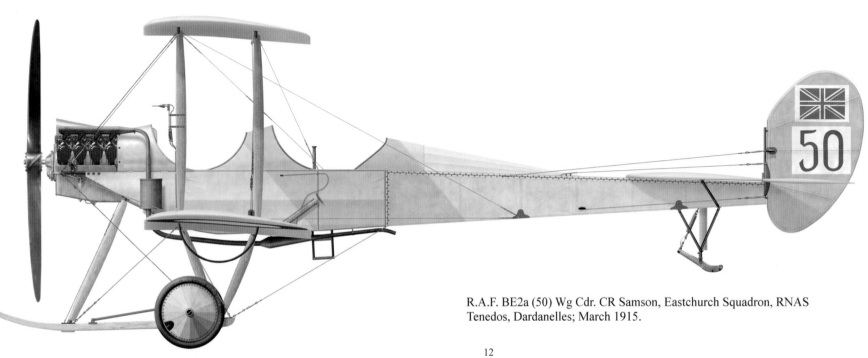

R.A.F. BE2a (50) Wg Cdr. CR Samson, Eastchurch Squadron, RNAS
Tenedos, Dardanelles; March 1915.

R.A.F. BE2b

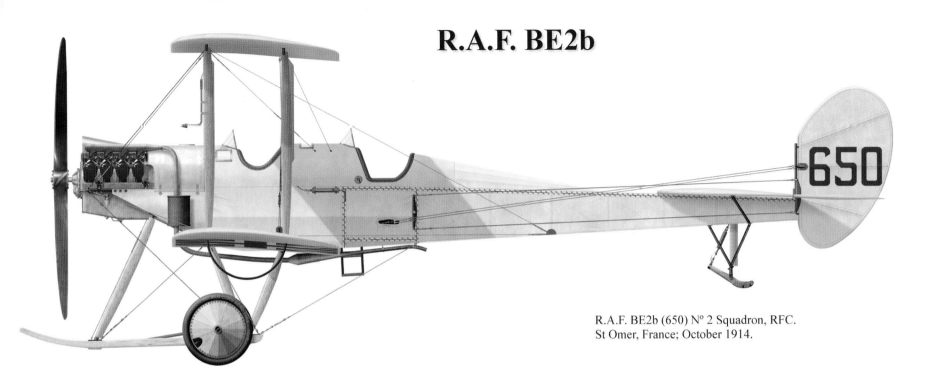

R.A.F. BE2b (650) Nº 2 Squadron, RFC.
St Omer, France; October 1914.

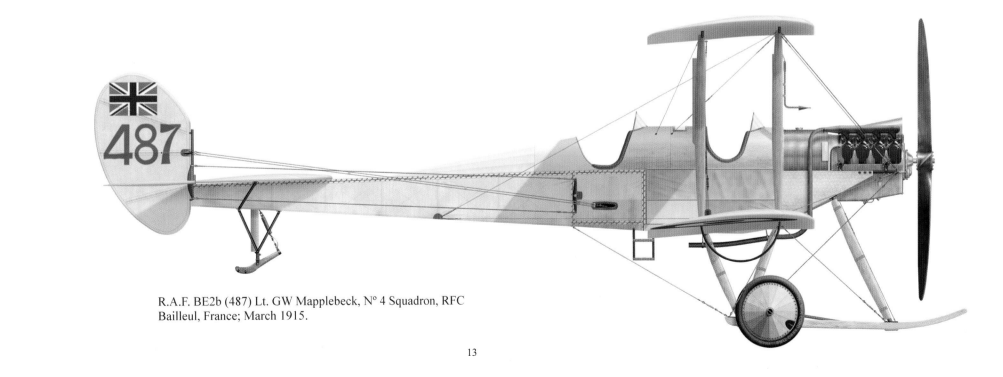

R.A.F. BE2b (487) Lt. GW Mapplebeck, Nº 4 Squadron, RFC
Bailleul, France; March 1915.

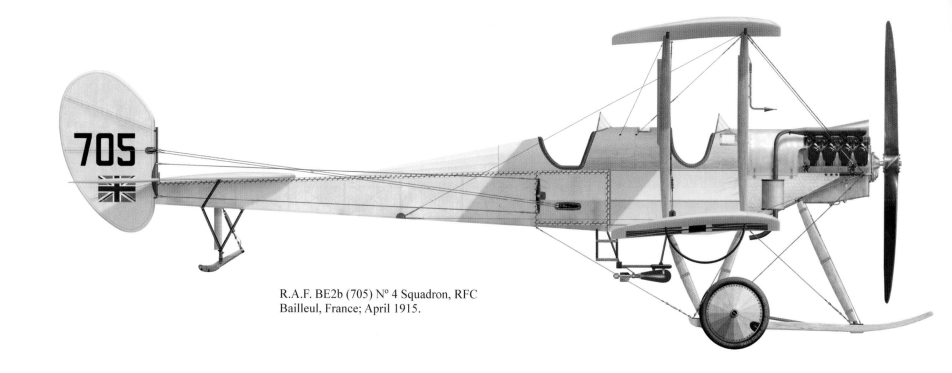

R.A.F. BE2b (705) Nº 4 Squadron, RFC
Bailleul, France; April 1915.

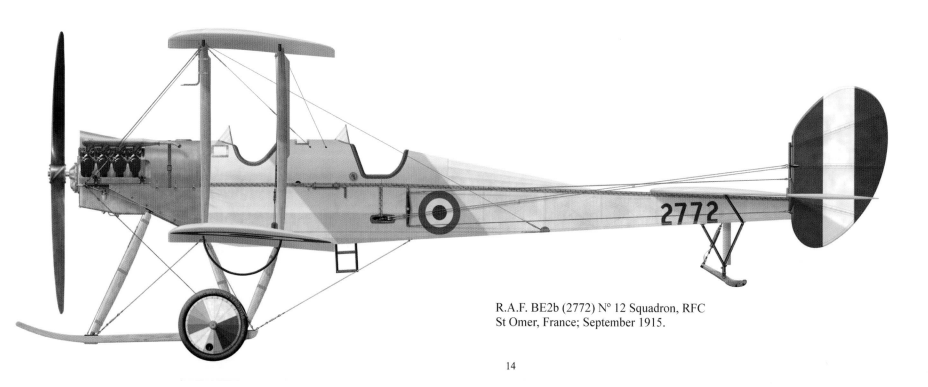

R.A.F. BE2b (2772) Nº 12 Squadron, RFC
St Omer, France; September 1915.

AVRO 504

AVRO 504 (874) Sqdn.Cdr. E Featherstone-Brigg, Special Detachment, RNAS
Belfort, France; November 1914.
One of the three aircraft that attacked the Friedrichshafen Zeppelin base at Lake Constance on 21-11-14.

AVRO 504 (753) 2Lt. Joubert de la Ferté & Lt. Dawyck MV Veitsch, Nº 1 Squadron, RFC
St Omer, France; March 1915.
Forced to land in the Netherlands on 21-3-15, after the engine was hit by AA fire.
Notice field applied camouflage.

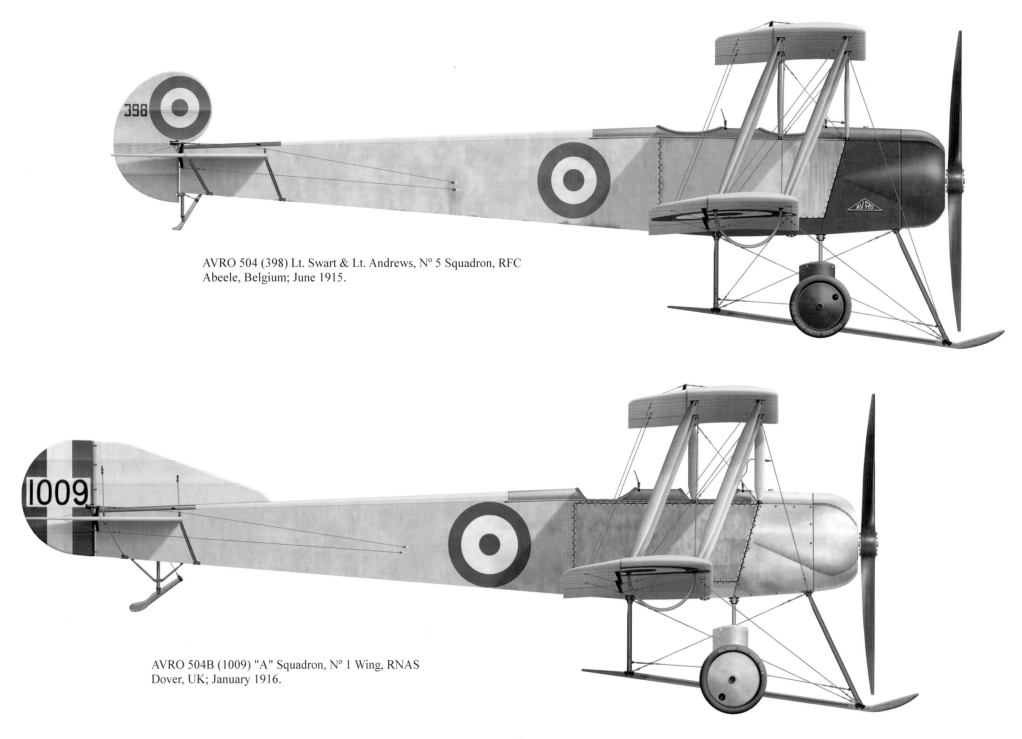

AVRO 504 (398) Lt. Swart & Lt. Andrews, Nº 5 Squadron, RFC
Abeele, Belgium; June 1915.

AVRO 504B (1009) "A" Squadron, Nº 1 Wing, RNAS
Dover, UK; January 1916.

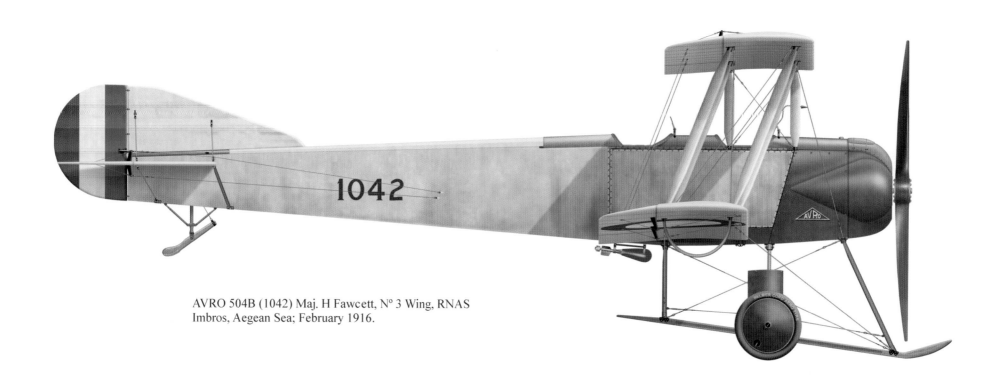

AVRO 504B (1042) Maj. H Fawcett, Nº 3 Wing, RNAS
Imbros, Aegean Sea; February 1916.

AVRO 504A (7991) Nº 65 (Reserve) Squadron, RFC
Sedgeford, UK; circa 1917.

AVRO 504A (A5921) School of Special Flying, RFC
Gosport, UK; circa 1917.

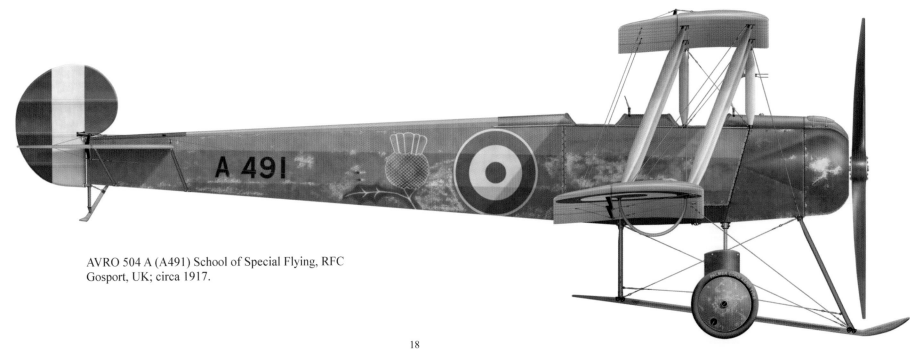

AVRO 504 A (A491) School of Special Flying, RFC
Gosport, UK; circa 1917.

AVRO 504B (B396) Nº 83 Squadron, RFC
Spittlegate, UK; July 1917.

AVRO 504J (B3155) "F" Flight, School of Special Flying, RFC
Gosport, UK; circa 1917.

AVRO 504J (B3165) "A" Flight, School of Special Flying, RFC
Gosport, UK; circa 1917.

AVRO 504K (D7617) Nº 94 Squadron, RAF
Harling Road, UK; June 1918.
Note the two Hythe camera guns, one on the top wing for the pilot and
the other on a Scarff ring for the observer.

AVRO 504J (C4393) South Eastern Area Flying Instructors School, RAF Sheerness, UK; June 1918.

AVRO 504J (D7789) Nº 8 Training Squadron, AFC Leighterton, UK; Summer 1918.

21

AVRO 504K (E1735) Nº 187 Night Training Squadron, RAF
Retford, UK; Late 1918.

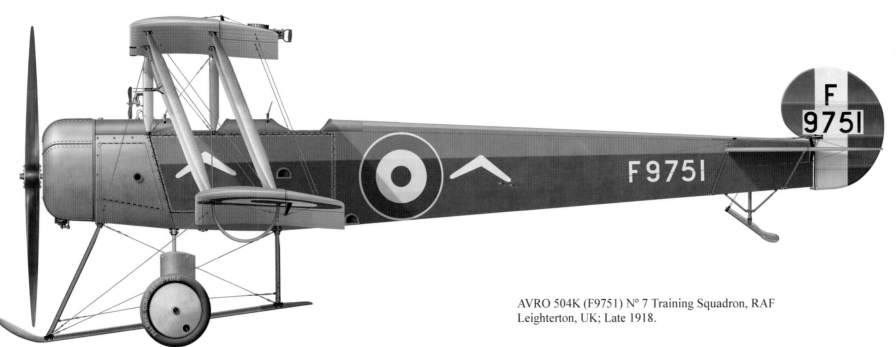

AVRO 504K (F9751) Nº 7 Training Squadron, RAF
Leighterton, UK; Late 1918.

22

R.A.F. BE2c

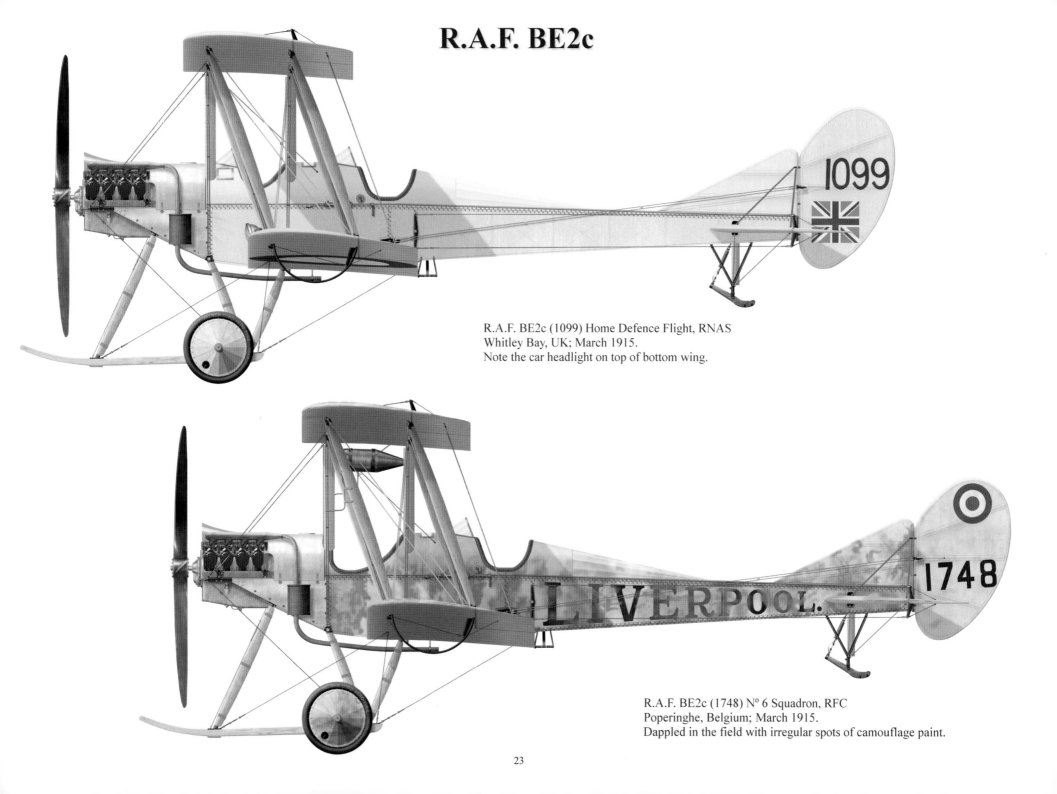

R.A.F. BE2c (1099) Home Defence Flight, RNAS
Whitley Bay, UK; March 1915.
Note the car headlight on top of bottom wing.

R.A.F. BE2c (1748) Nº 6 Squadron, RFC
Poperinghe, Belgium; March 1915.
Dappled in the field with irregular spots of camouflage paint.

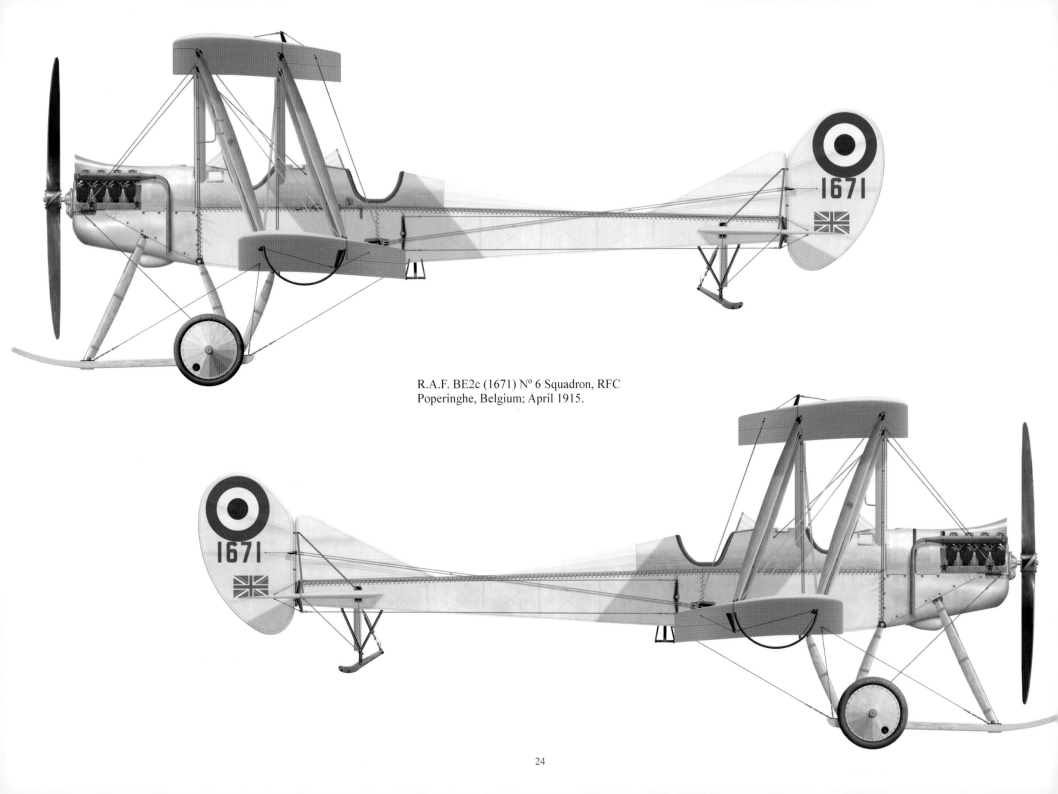

R.A.F. BE2c (1671) Nº 6 Squadron, RFC
Poperinghe, Belgium; April 1915.

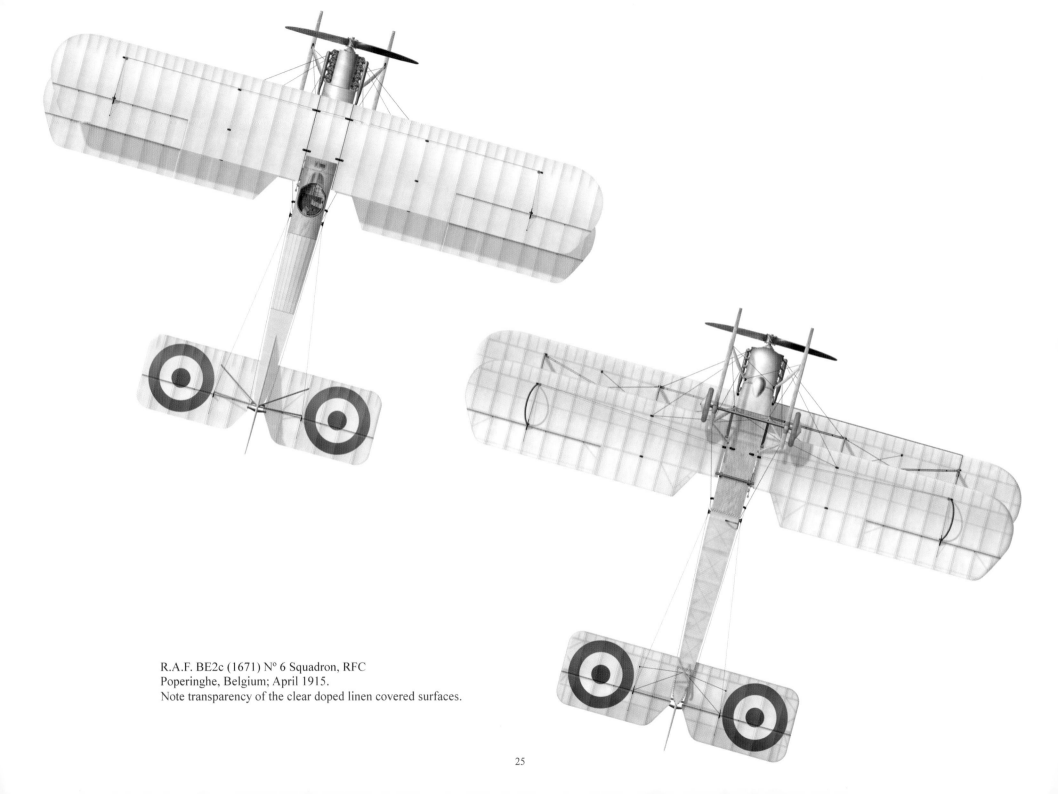

R.A.F. BE2c (1671) Nº 6 Squadron, RFC
Poperinghe, Belgium; April 1915.
Note transparency of the clear doped linen covered surfaces.

25

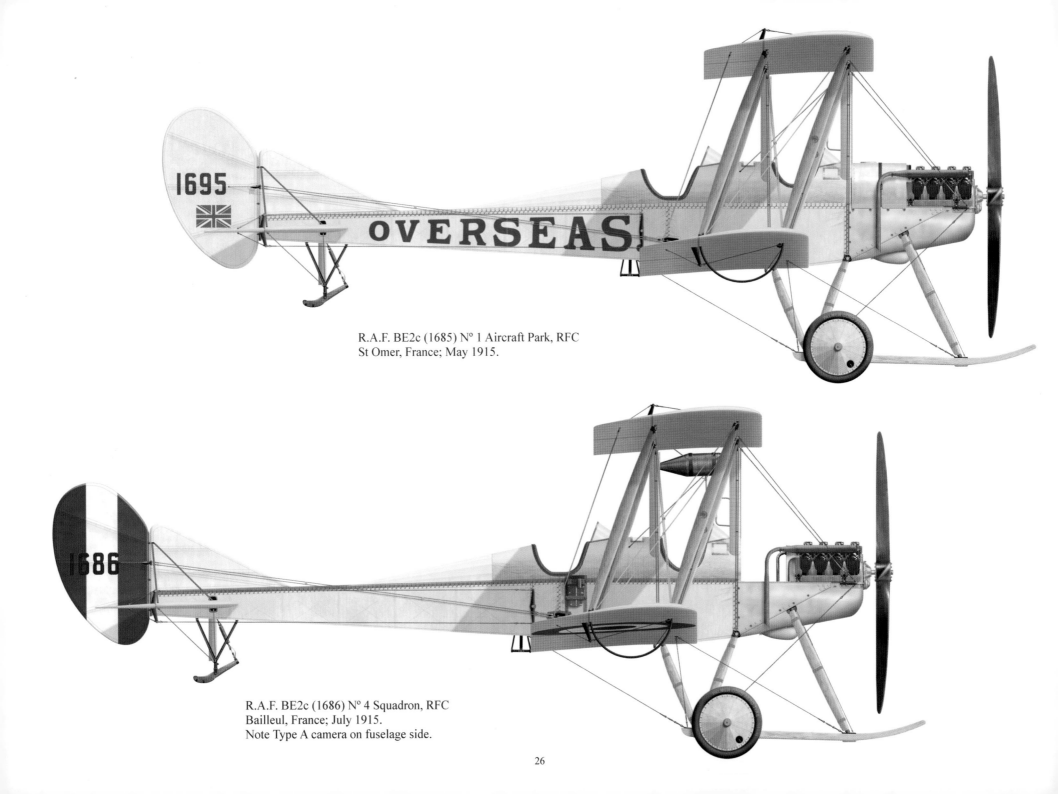

R.A.F. BE2c (1685) Nº 1 Aircraft Park, RFC
St Omer, France; May 1915.

R.A.F. BE2c (1686) Nº 4 Squadron, RFC
Bailleul, France; July 1915.
Note Type A camera on fuselage side.

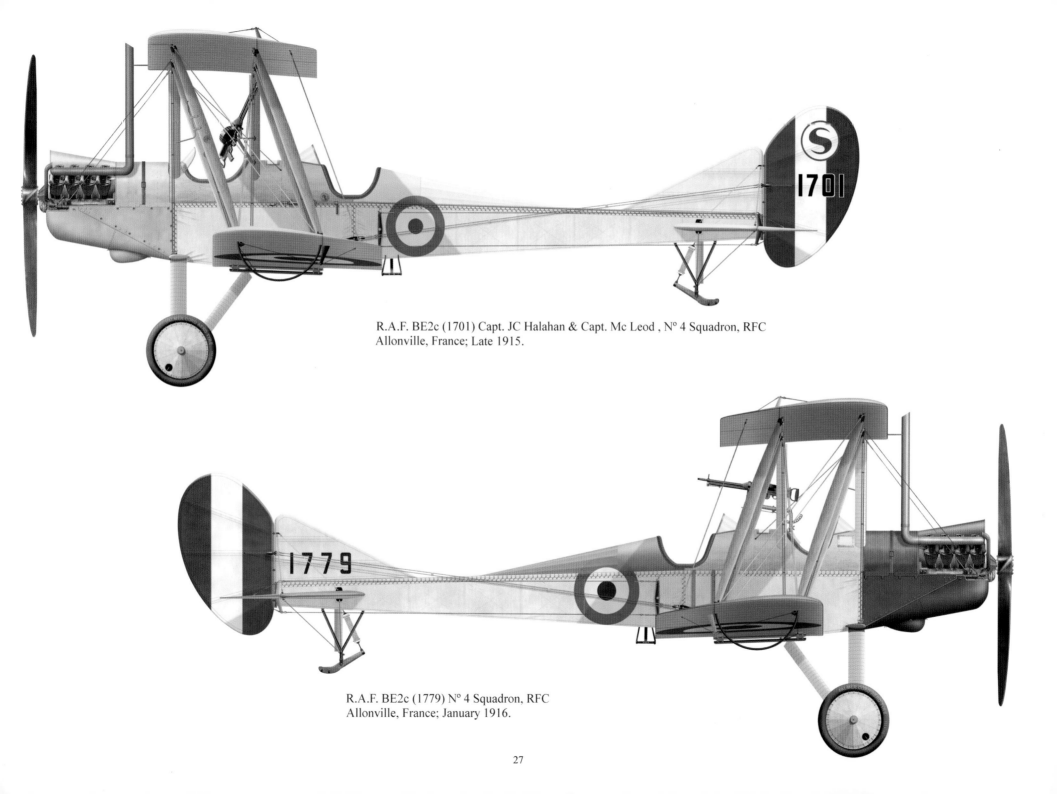

R.A.F. BE2c (1701) Capt. JC Halahan & Capt. Mc Leod , Nº 4 Squadron, RFC
Allonville, France; Late 1915.

R.A.F. BE2c (1779) Nº 4 Squadron, RFC
Allonville, France; January 1916.

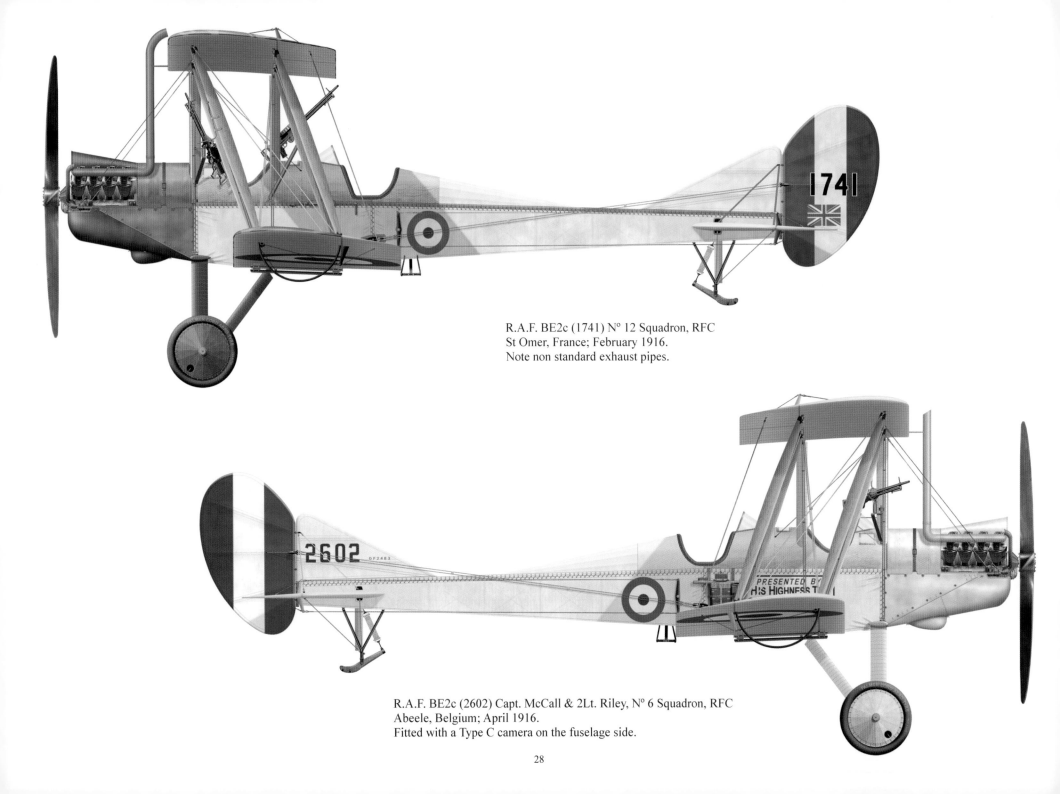

R.A.F. BE2c (1741) Nº 12 Squadron, RFC
St Omer, France; February 1916.
Note non standard exhaust pipes.

R.A.F. BE2c (2602) Capt. McCall & 2Lt. Riley, Nº 6 Squadron, RFC
Abeele, Belgium; April 1916.
Fitted with a Type C camera on the fuselage side.

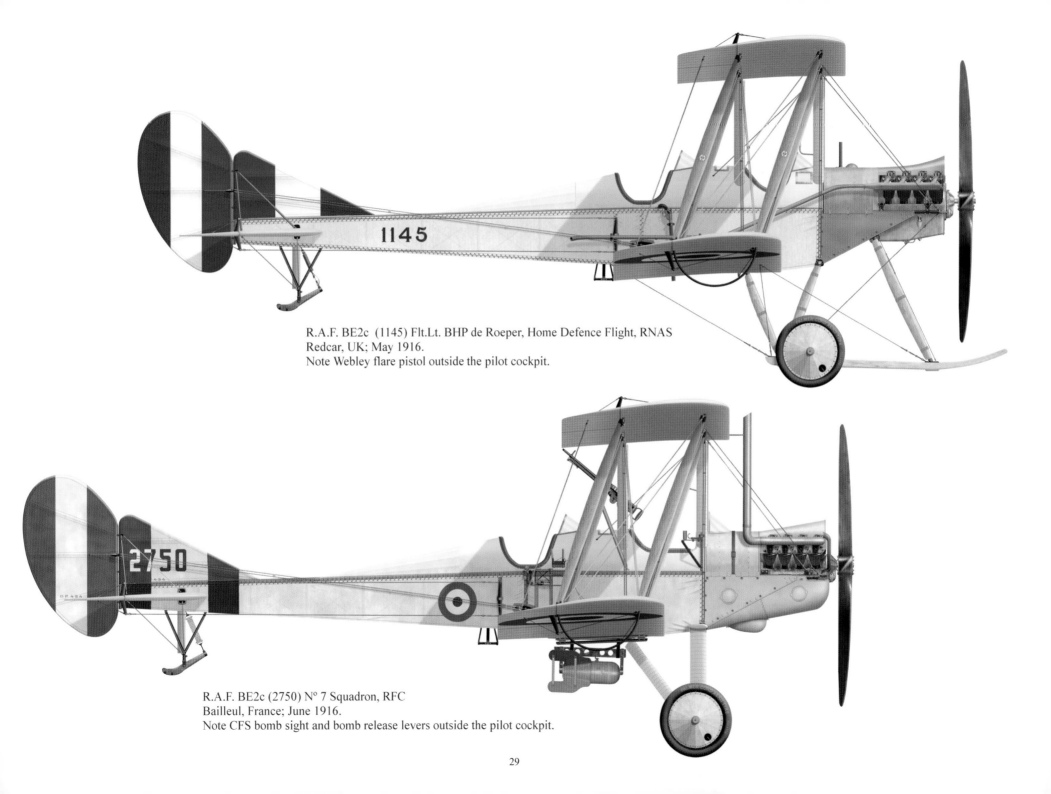

R.A.F. BE2c (1145) Flt.Lt. BHP de Roeper, Home Defence Flight, RNAS
Redcar, UK; May 1916.
Note Webley flare pistol outside the pilot cockpit.

R.A.F. BE2c (2750) Nº 7 Squadron, RFC
Bailleul, France; June 1916.
Note CFS bomb sight and bomb release levers outside the pilot cockpit.

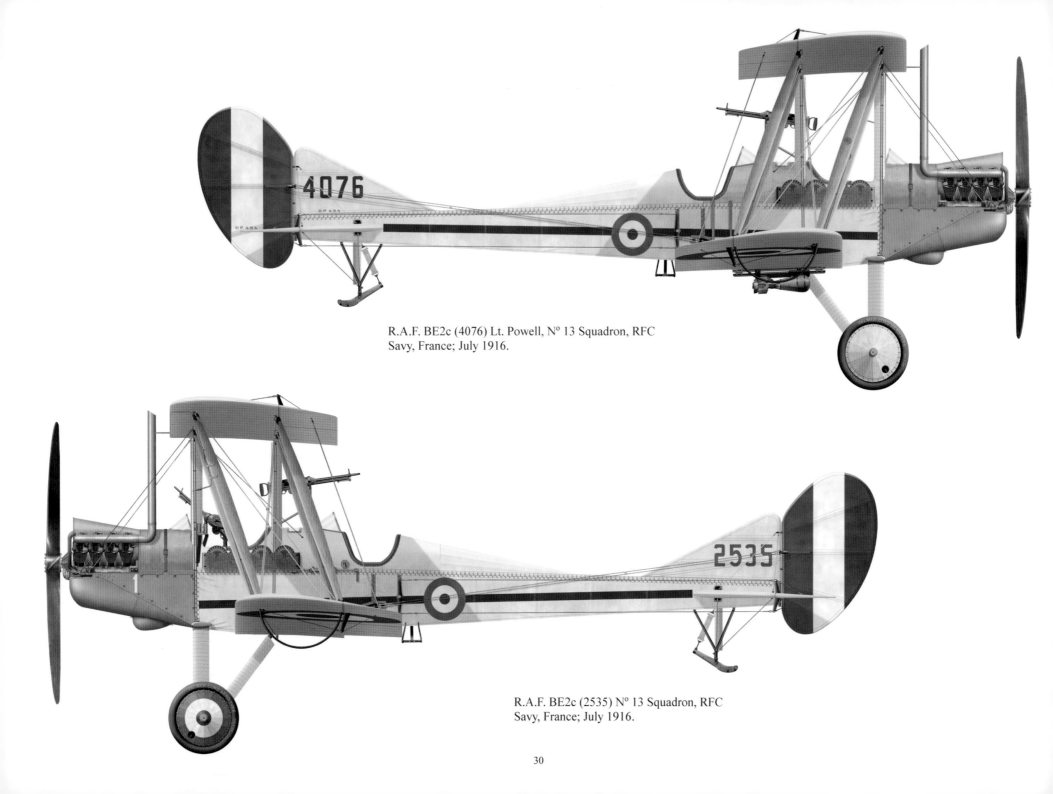

R.A.F. BE2c (4076) Lt. Powell, Nº 13 Squadron, RFC
Savy, France; July 1916.

R.A.F. BE2c (2535) Nº 13 Squadron, RFC
Savy, France; July 1916.

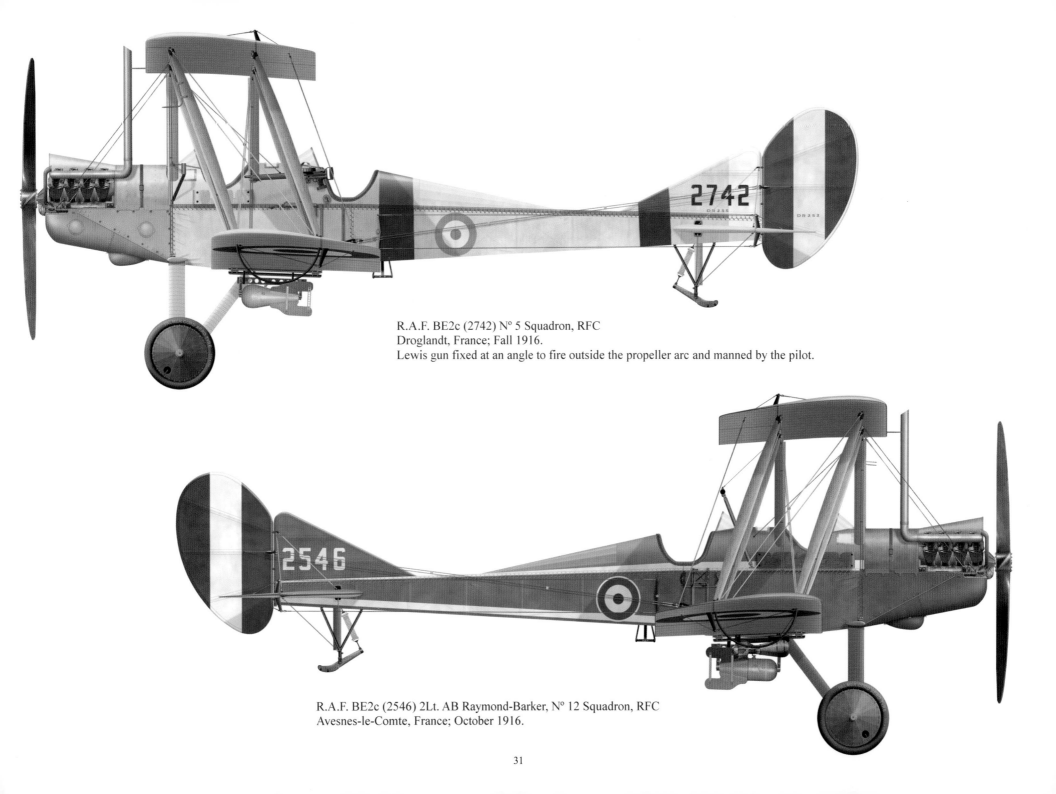

R.A.F. BE2c (2742) Nº 5 Squadron, RFC
Droglandt, France; Fall 1916.
Lewis gun fixed at an angle to fire outside the propeller arc and manned by the pilot.

R.A.F. BE2c (2546) 2Lt. AB Raymond-Barker, Nº 12 Squadron, RFC
Avesnes-le-Comte, France; October 1916.

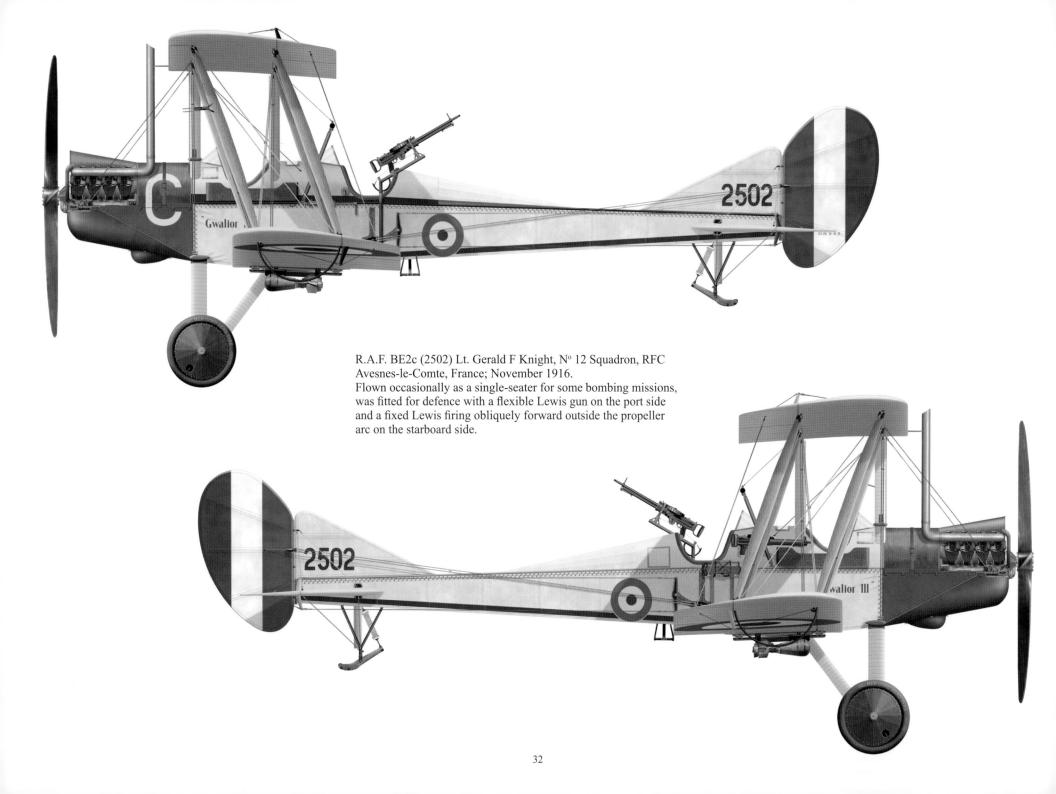

R.A.F. BE2c (2502) Lt. Gerald F Knight, Nº 12 Squadron, RFC
Avesnes-le-Comte, France; November 1916.
Flown occasionally as a single-seater for some bombing missions,
was fitted for defence with a flexible Lewis gun on the port side
and a fixed Lewis firing obliquely forward outside the propeller
arc on the starboard side.

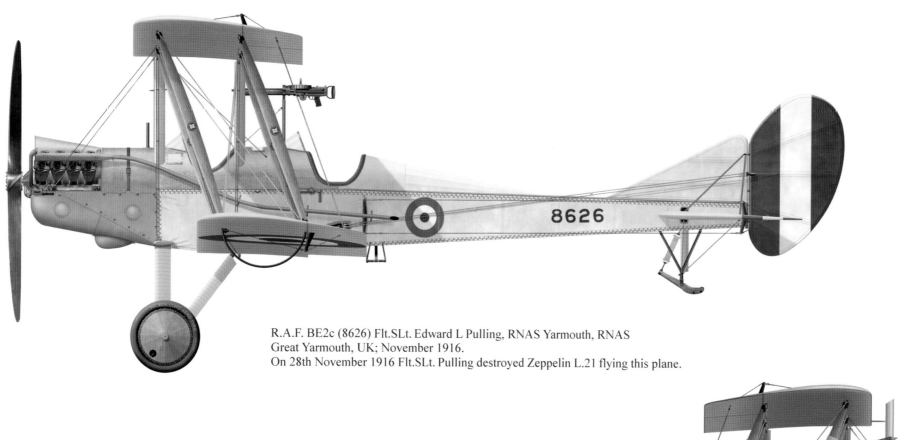

R.A.F. BE2c (8626) Flt.SLt. Edward L Pulling, RNAS Yarmouth, RNAS
Great Yarmouth, UK; November 1916.
On 28th November 1916 Flt.SLt. Pulling destroyed Zeppelin L.21 flying this plane.

R.A.F. BE2c (8407) RNAS East Fortune, RNAS
East Lothian, UK; December 1916.
Armed with Le Prieur rockets for anti-Zeppelin work.

R.A.F. BE2d

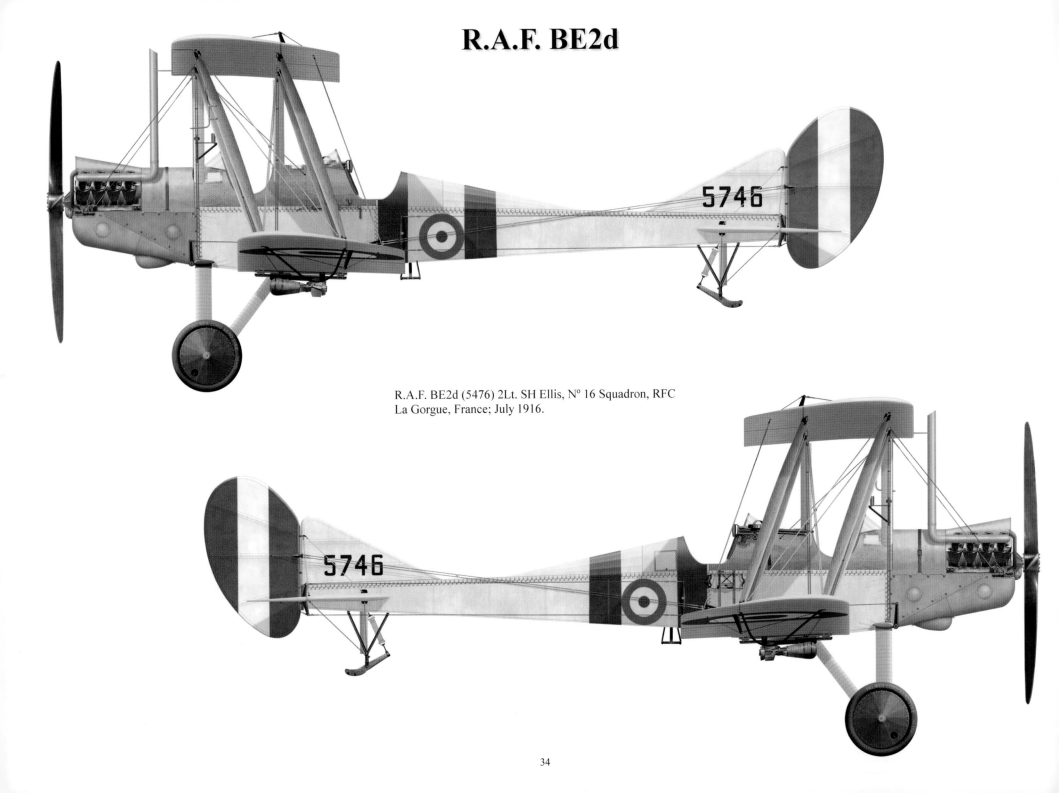

R.A.F. BE2d (5476) 2Lt. SH Ellis, N° 16 Squadron, RFC
La Gorgue, France; July 1916.

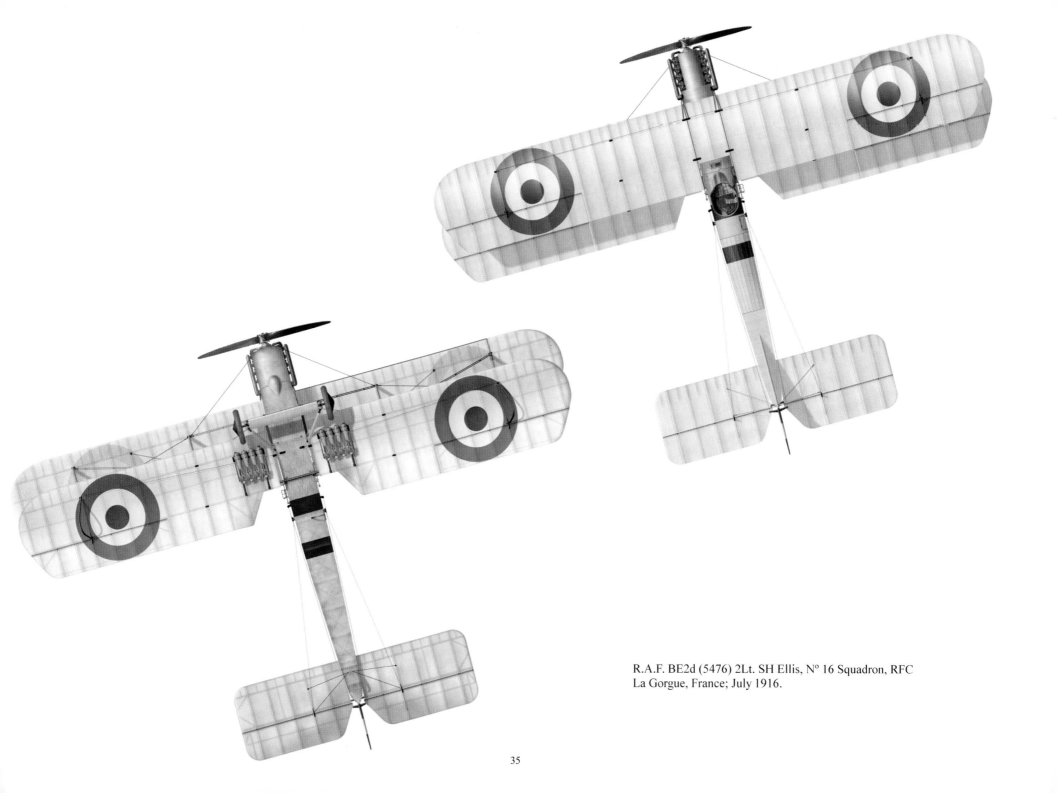

R.A.F. BE2d (5476) 2Lt. SH Ellis, Nº 16 Squadron, RFC
La Gorgue, France; July 1916.

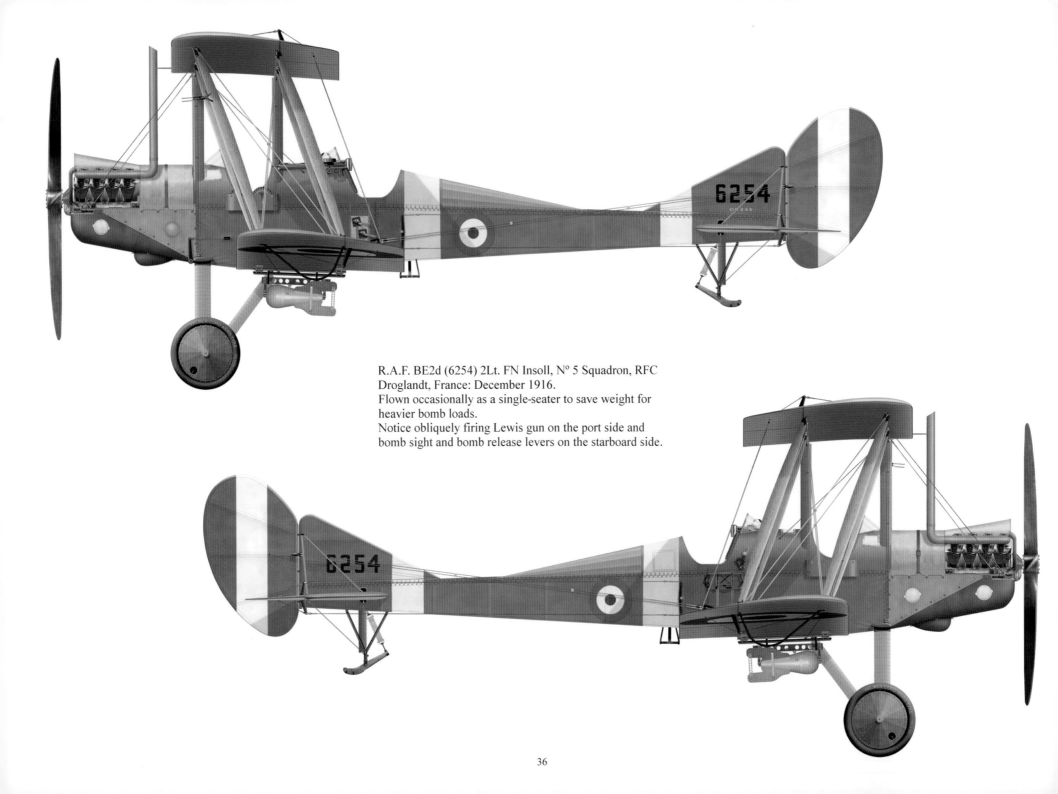

R.A.F. BE2d (6254) 2Lt. FN Insoll, N° 5 Squadron, RFC
Droglandt, France: December 1916.
Flown occasionally as a single-seater to save weight for
heavier bomb loads.
Notice obliquely firing Lewis gun on the port side and
bomb sight and bomb release levers on the starboard side.

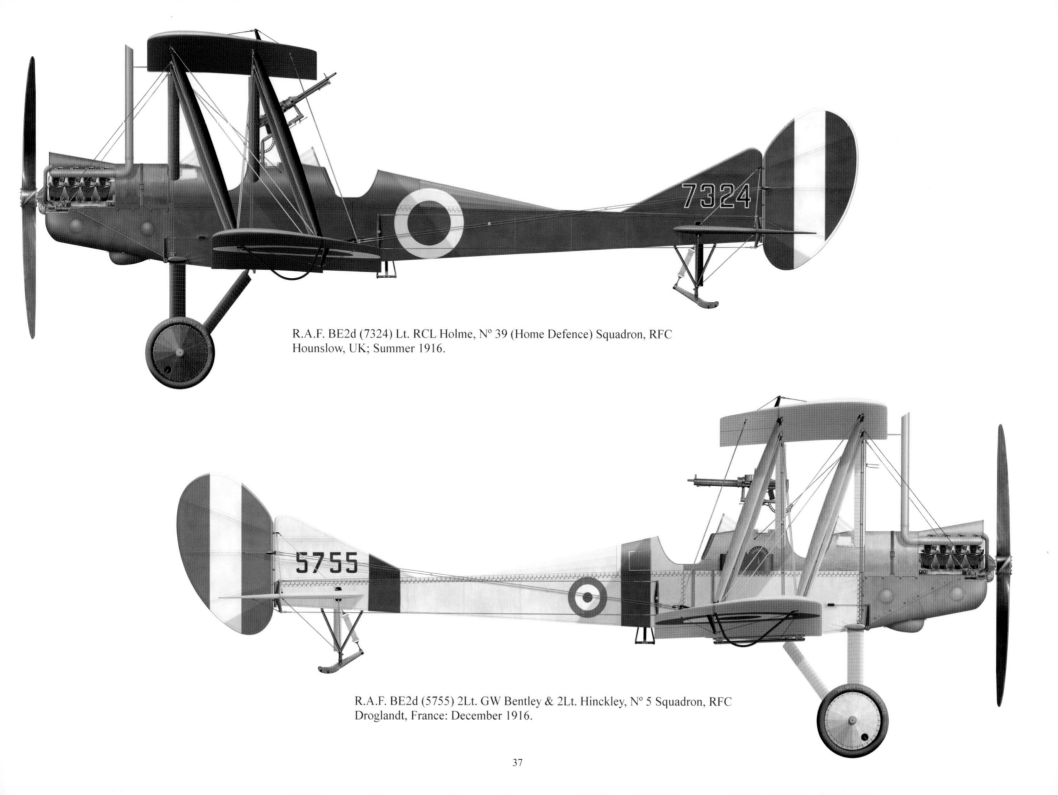

R.A.F. BE2d (7324) Lt. RCL Holme, Nº 39 (Home Defence) Squadron, RFC
Hounslow, UK; Summer 1916.

R.A.F. BE2d (5755) 2Lt. GW Bentley & 2Lt. Hinckley, Nº 5 Squadron, RFC
Droglandt, France: December 1916.

VICKERS FB5

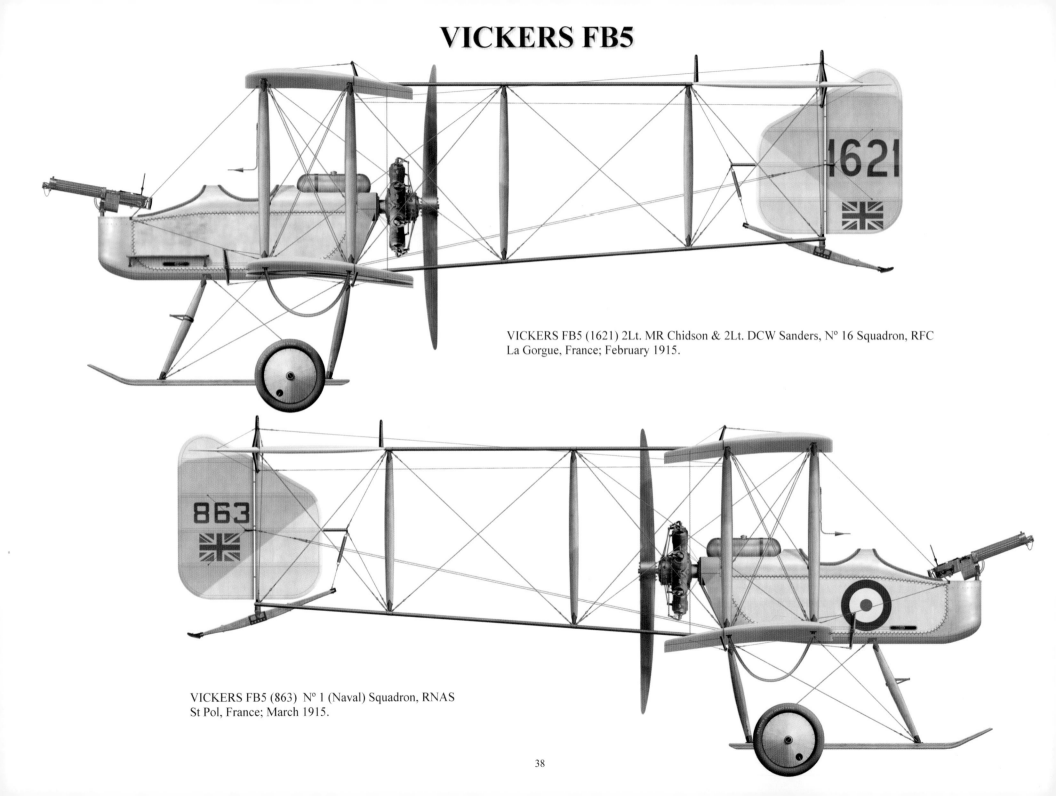

VICKERS FB5 (1621) 2Lt. MR Chidson & 2Lt. DCW Sanders, Nº 16 Squadron, RFC
La Gorgue, France; February 1915.

VICKERS FB5 (863) Nº 1 (Naval) Squadron, RNAS
St Pol, France; March 1915.

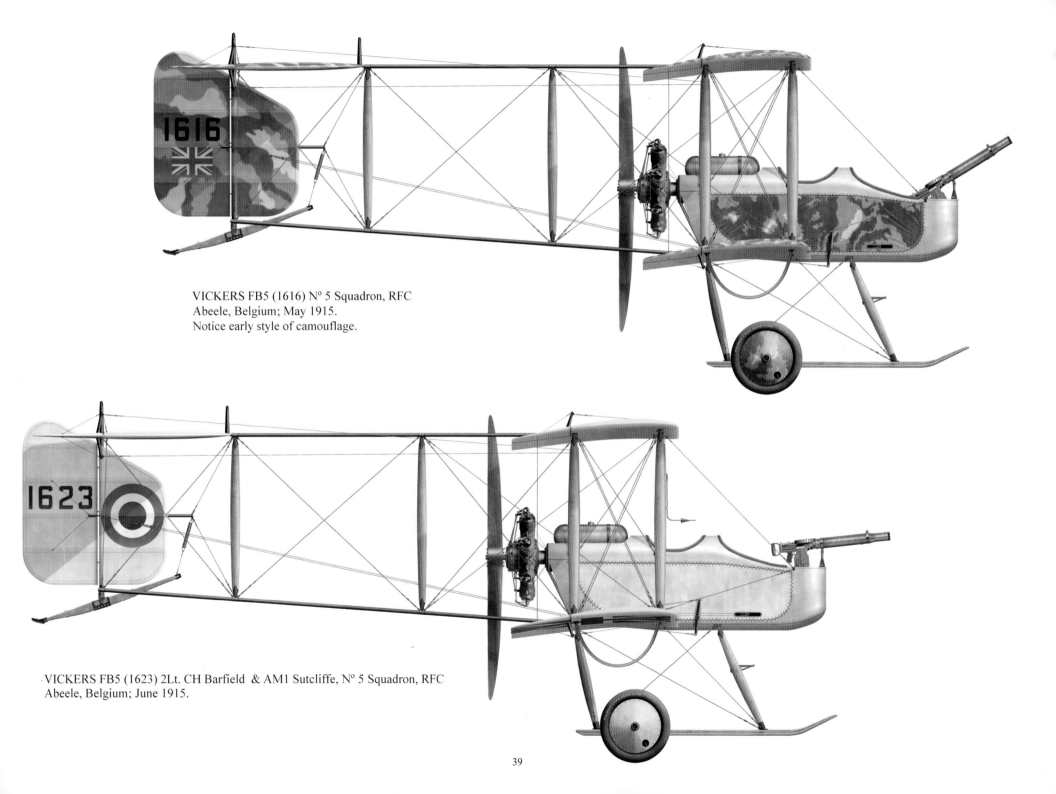

VICKERS FB5 (1616) Nº 5 Squadron, RFC
Abeele, Belgium; May 1915.
Notice early style of camouflage.

VICKERS FB5 (1623) 2Lt. CH Barfield & AM1 Sutcliffe, Nº 5 Squadron, RFC
Abeele, Belgium; June 1915.

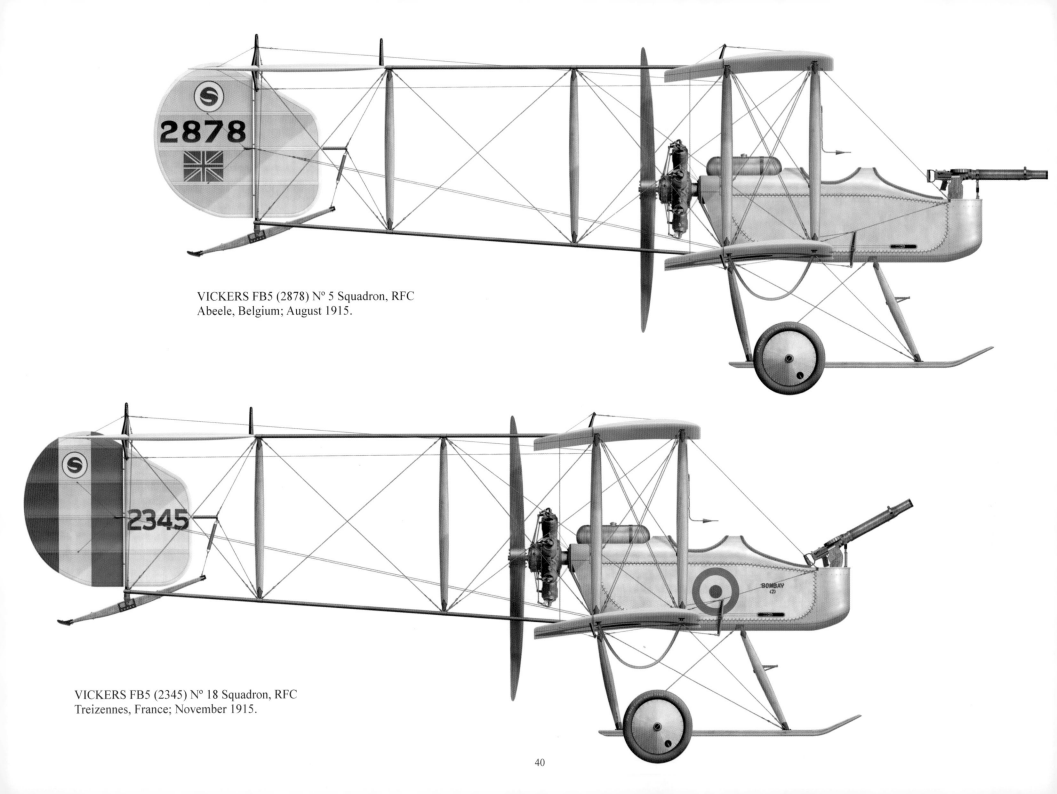

VICKERS FB5 (2878) Nº 5 Squadron, RFC
Abeele, Belgium; August 1915.

VICKERS FB5 (2345) Nº 18 Squadron, RFC
Treizennes, France; November 1915.

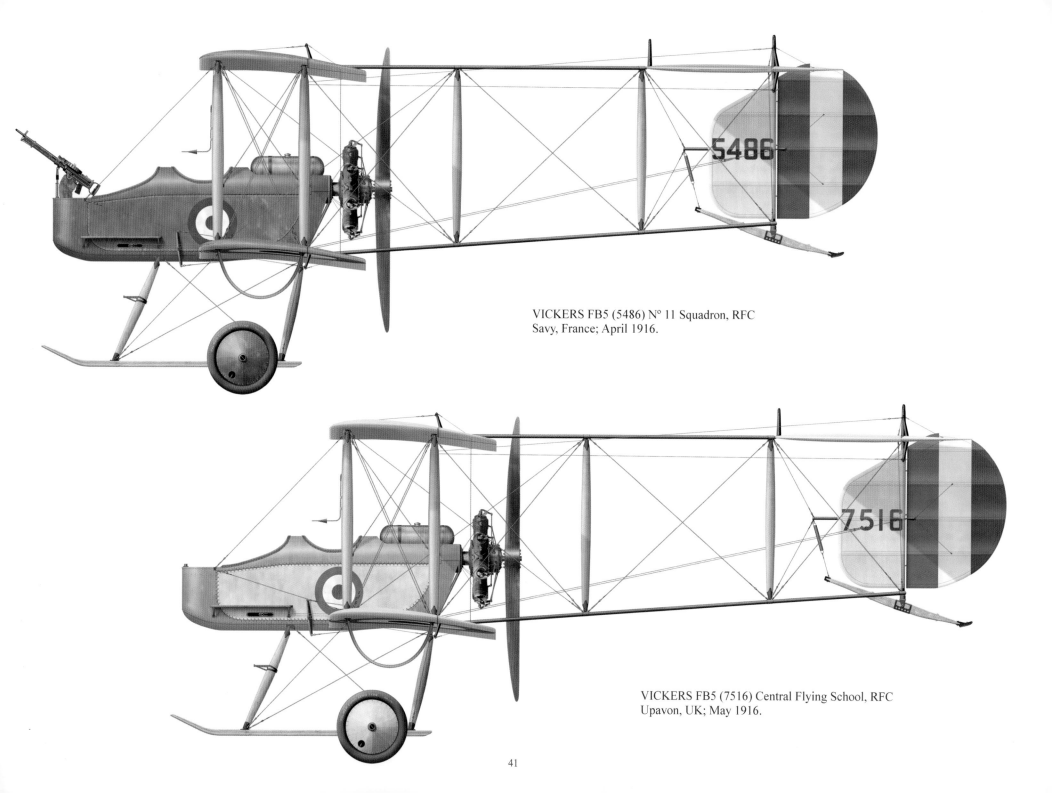

VICKERS FB5 (5486) N° 11 Squadron, RFC
Savy, France; April 1916.

VICKERS FB5 (7516) Central Flying School, RFC
Upavon, UK; May 1916.

R.A.F. FE2b

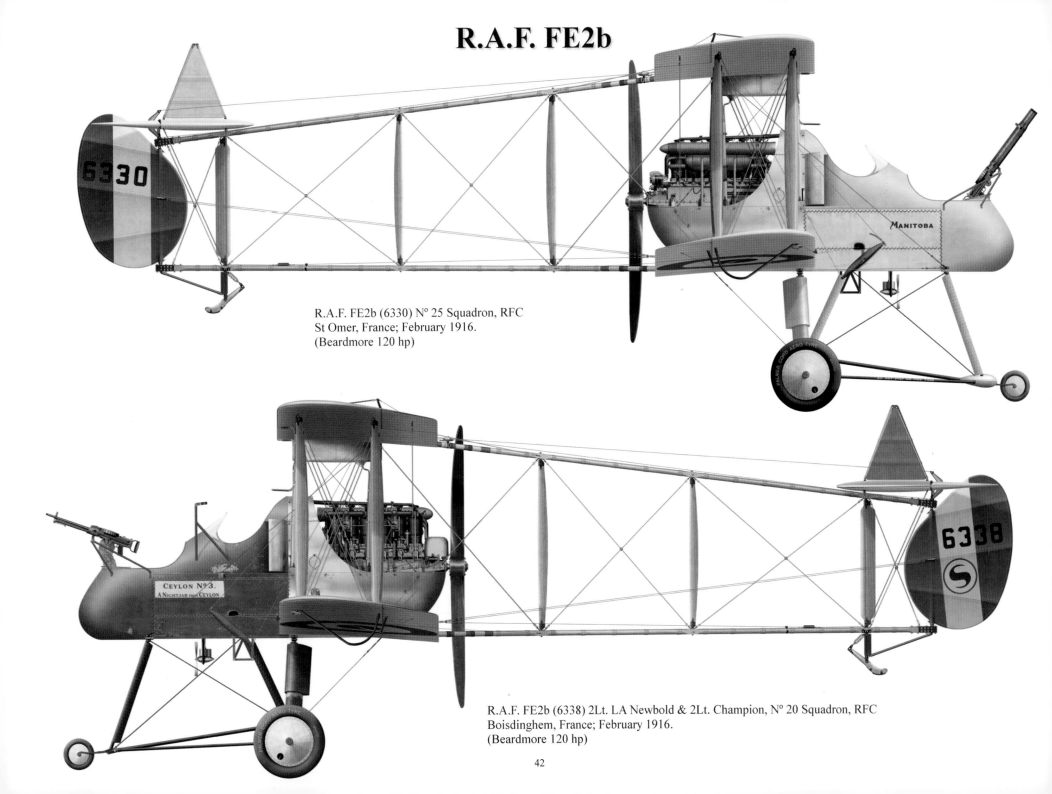

R.A.F. FE2b (6330) N° 25 Squadron, RFC
St Omer, France; February 1916.
(Beardmore 120 hp)

R.A.F. FE2b (6338) 2Lt. LA Newbold & 2Lt. Champion, N° 20 Squadron, RFC
Boisdinghem, France; February 1916.
(Beardmore 120 hp)

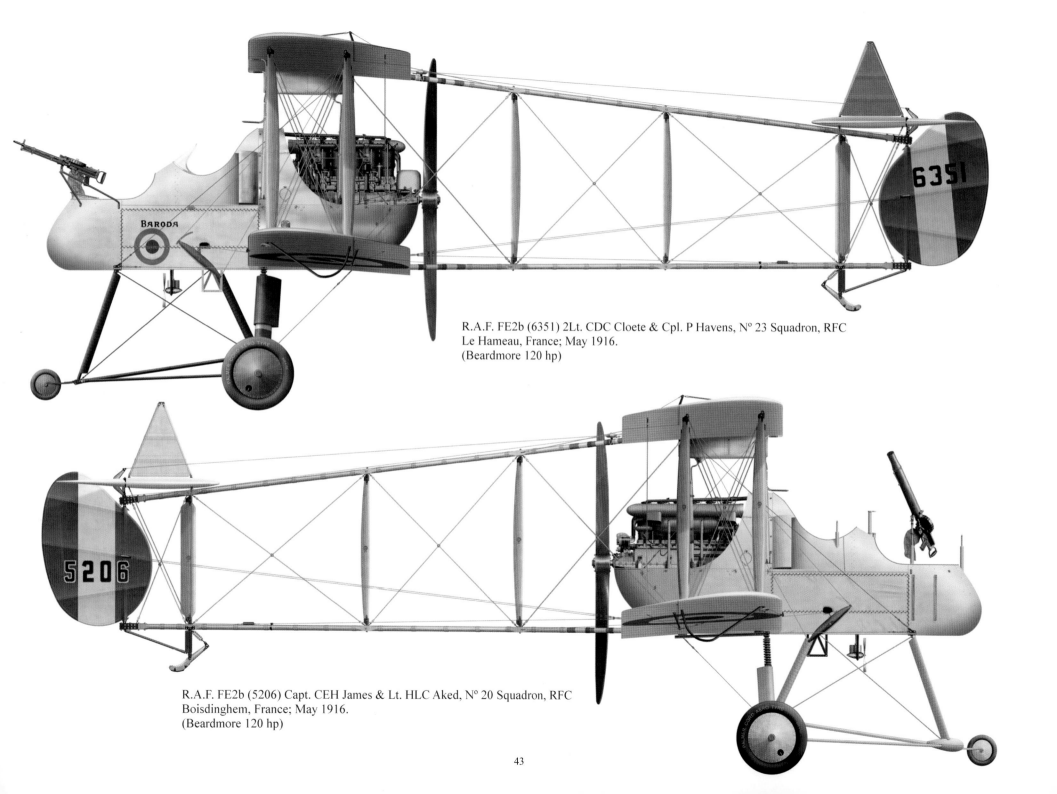

R.A.F. FE2b (6351) 2Lt. CDC Cloete & Cpl. P Havens, Nº 23 Squadron, RFC
Le Hameau, France; May 1916.
(Beardmore 120 hp)

R.A.F. FE2b (5206) Capt. CEH James & Lt. HLC Aked, Nº 20 Squadron, RFC
Boisdinghem, France; May 1916.
(Beardmore 120 hp)

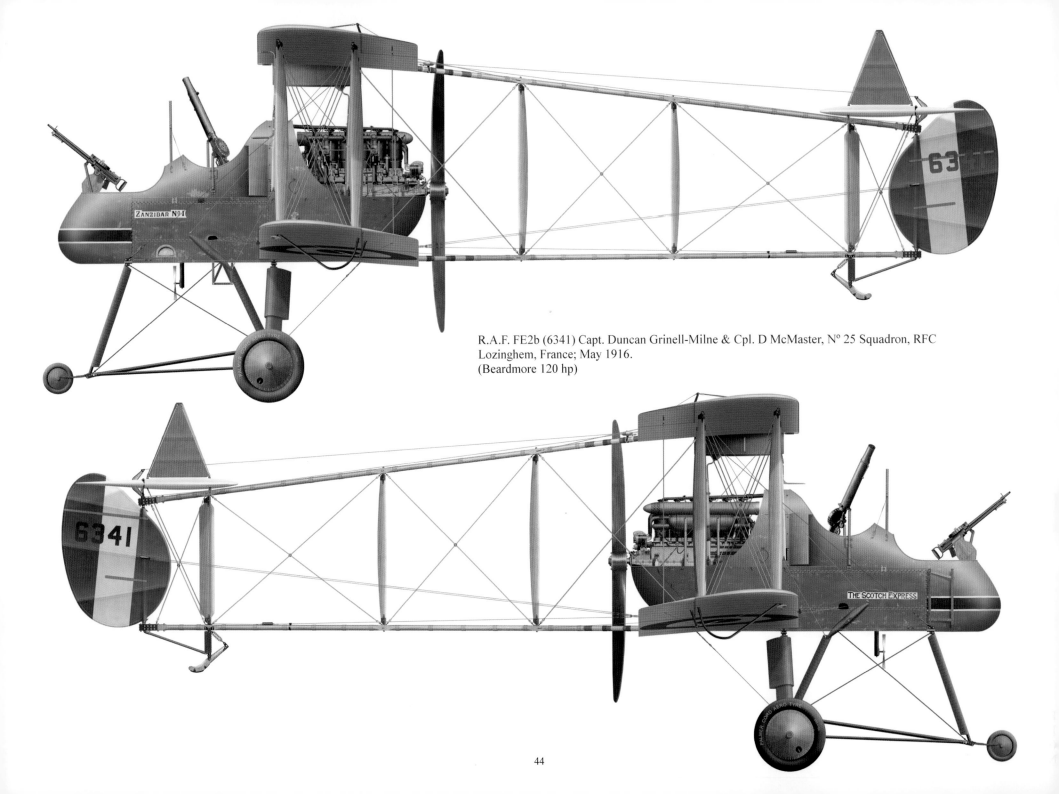

R.A.F. FE2b (6341) Capt. Duncan Grinell-Milne & Cpl. D McMaster, Nº 25 Squadron, RFC
Lozinghem, France; May 1916.
(Beardmore 120 hp)

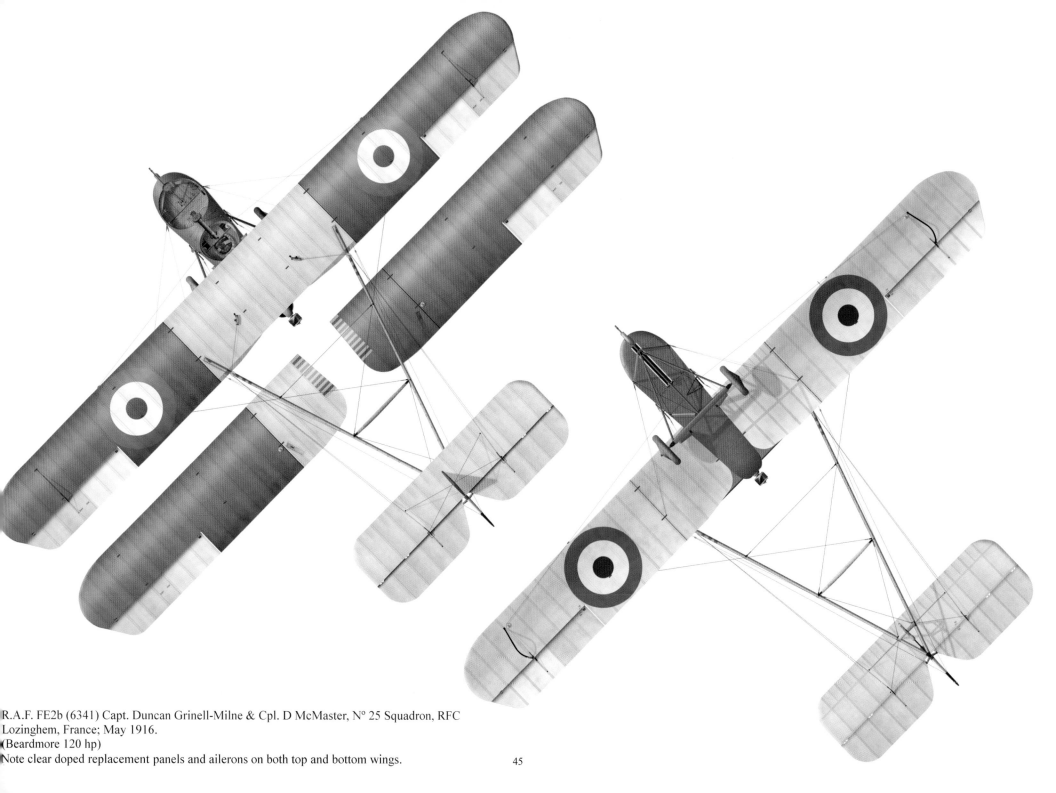

R.A.F. FE2b (6341) Capt. Duncan Grinell-Milne & Cpl. D McMaster, Nº 25 Squadron, RFC
Lozinghem, France; May 1916.
(Beardmore 120 hp)
Note clear doped replacement panels and ailerons on both top and bottom wings.

45

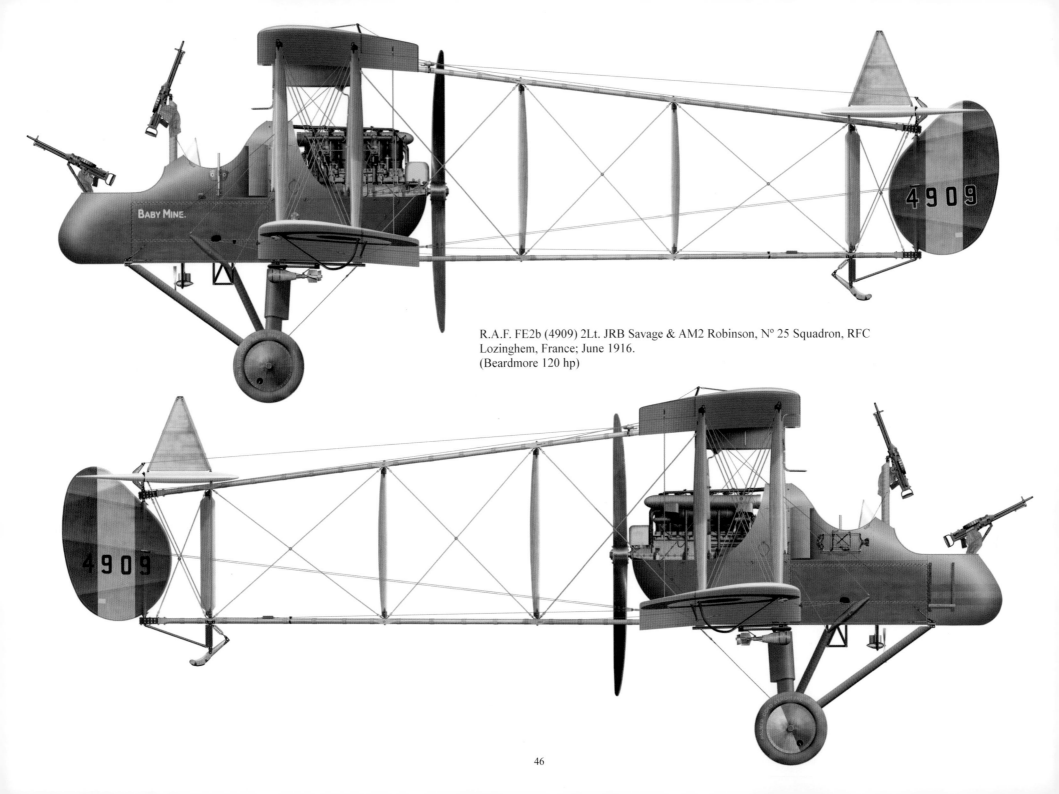

R.A.F. FE2b (4909) 2Lt. JRB Savage & AM2 Robinson, Nº 25 Squadron, RFC
Lozinghem, France; June 1916.
(Beardmore 120 hp)

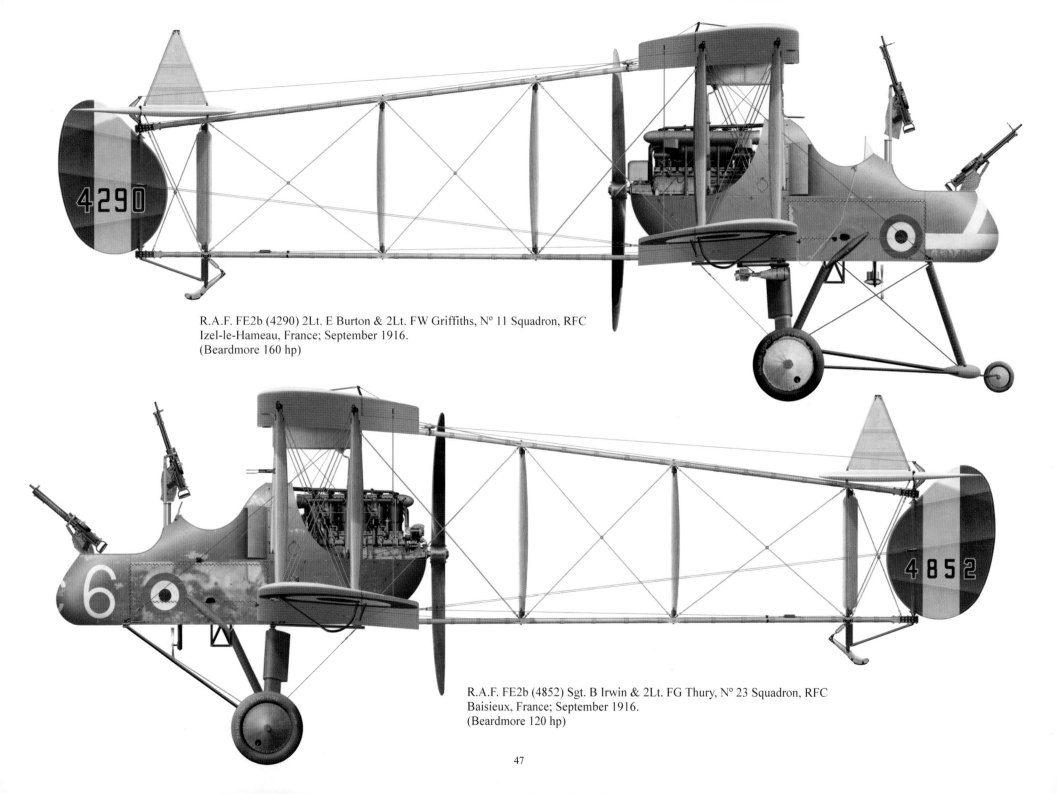

R.A.F. FE2b (4290) 2Lt. E Burton & 2Lt. FW Griffiths, Nº 11 Squadron, RFC
Izel-le-Hameau, France; September 1916.
(Beardmore 160 hp)

R.A.F. FE2b (4852) Sgt. B Irwin & 2Lt. FG Thury, Nº 23 Squadron, RFC
Baisieux, France; September 1916.
(Beardmore 120 hp)

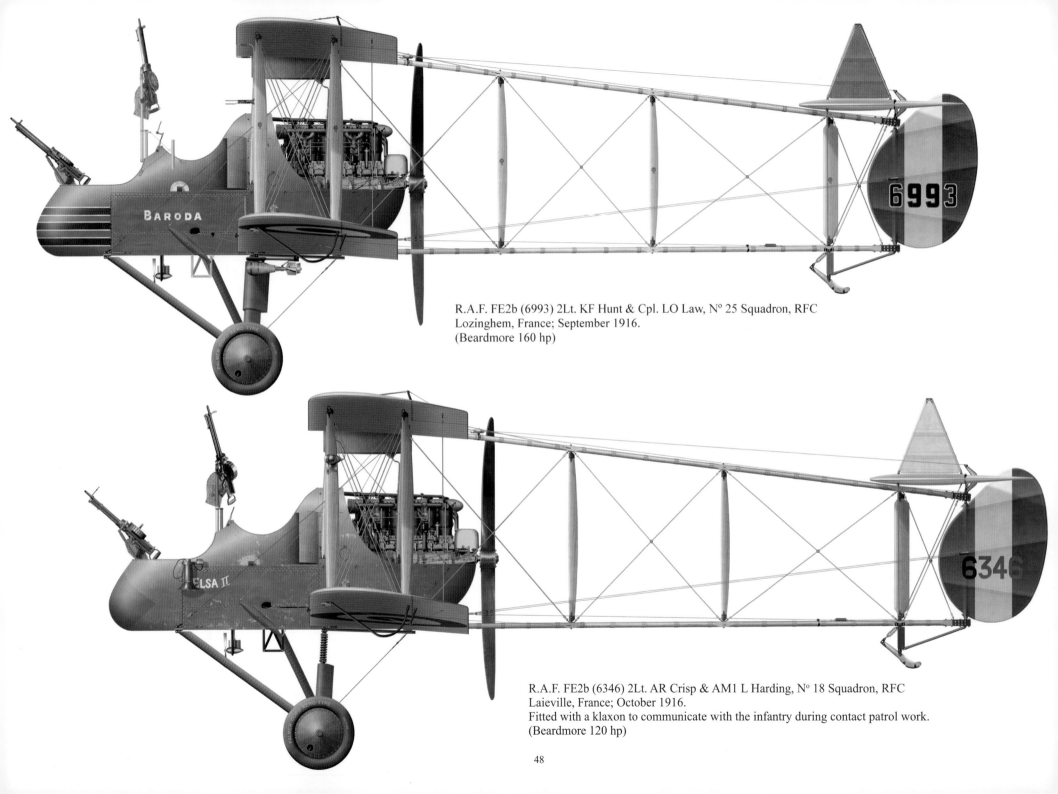

R.A.F. FE2b (6993) 2Lt. KF Hunt & Cpl. LO Law, Nº 25 Squadron, RFC
Lozinghem, France; September 1916.
(Beardmore 160 hp)

R.A.F. FE2b (6346) 2Lt. AR Crisp & AM1 L Harding, Nº 18 Squadron, RFC
Laieville, France; October 1916.
Fitted with a klaxon to communicate with the infantry during contact patrol work.
(Beardmore 120 hp)

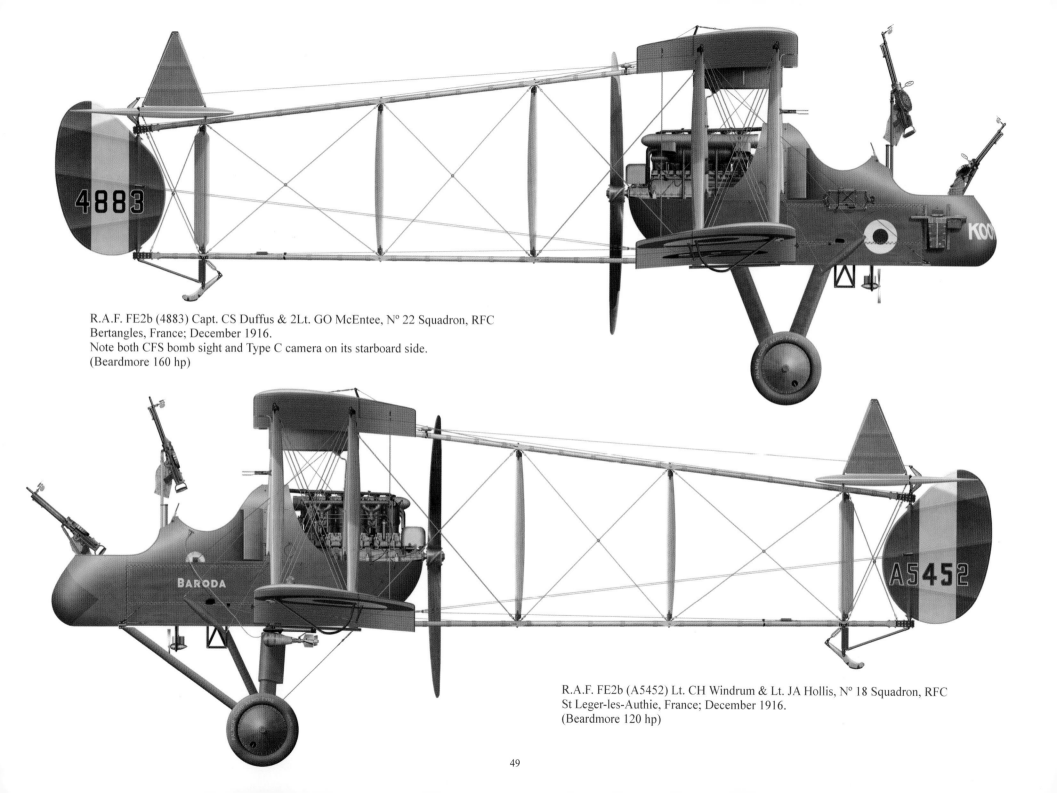

R.A.F. FE2b (4883) Capt. CS Duffus & 2Lt. GO McEntee, Nº 22 Squadron, RFC
Bertangles, France; December 1916.
Note both CFS bomb sight and Type C camera on its starboard side.
(Beardmore 160 hp)

R.A.F. FE2b (A5452) Lt. CH Windrum & Lt. JA Hollis, Nº 18 Squadron, RFC
St Leger-les-Authie, France; December 1916.
(Beardmore 120 hp)

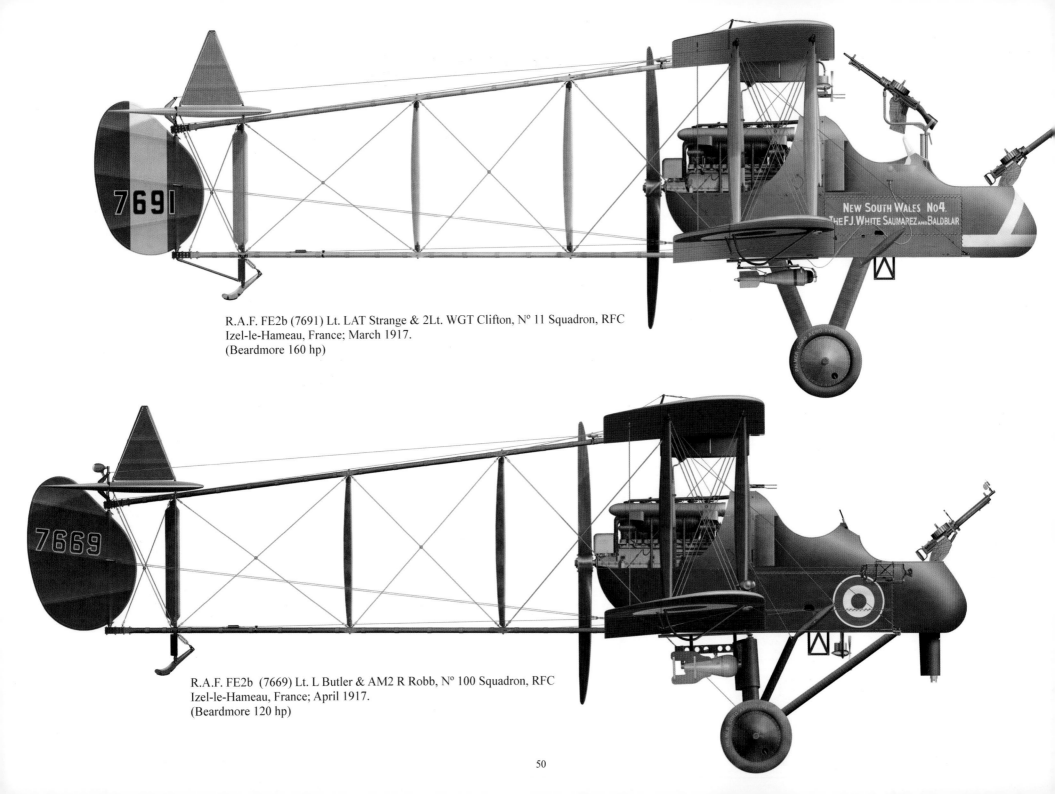

R.A.F. FE2b (7691) Lt. LAT Strange & 2Lt. WGT Clifton, Nº 11 Squadron, RFC
Izel-le-Hameau, France; March 1917.
(Beardmore 160 hp)

NEW SOUTH WALES Nº4.
THE F.J. WHITE SAUMAREZ AND BALDBLAIR

R.A.F. FE2b (7669) Lt. L Butler & AM2 R Robb, Nº 100 Squadron, RFC
Izel-le-Hameau, France; April 1917.
(Beardmore 120 hp)

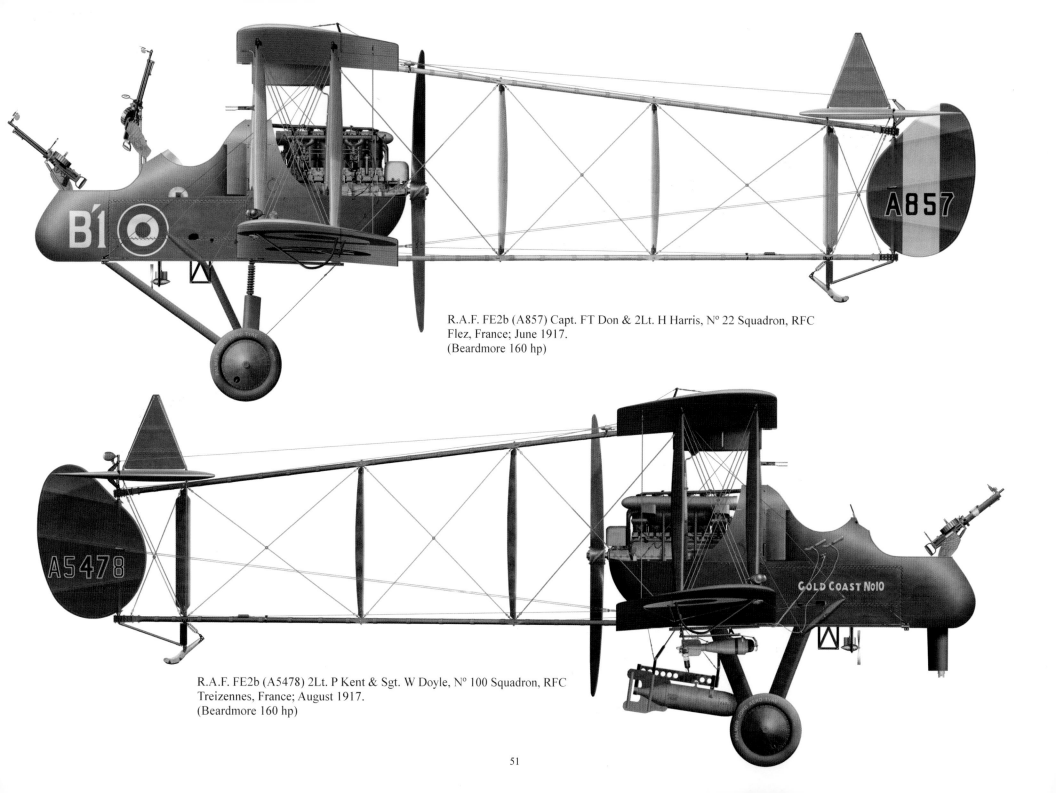

R.A.F. FE2b (A857) Capt. FT Don & 2Lt. H Harris, Nº 22 Squadron, RFC
Flez, France; June 1917.
(Beardmore 160 hp)

R.A.F. FE2b (A5478) 2Lt. P Kent & Sgt. W Doyle, Nº 100 Squadron, RFC
Treizennes, France; August 1917.
(Beardmore 160 hp)

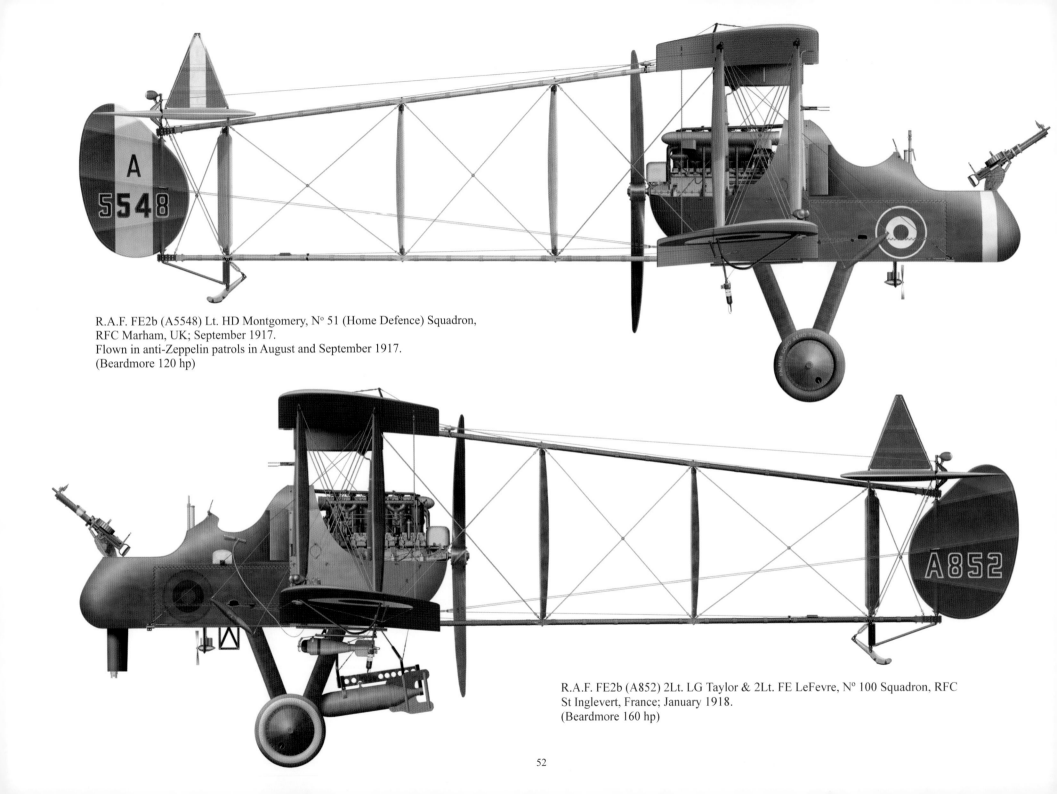

R.A.F. FE2b (A5548) Lt. HD Montgomery, N° 51 (Home Defence) Squadron,
RFC Marham, UK; September 1917.
Flown in anti-Zeppelin patrols in August and September 1917.
(Beardmore 120 hp)

R.A.F. FE2b (A852) 2Lt. LG Taylor & 2Lt. FE LeFevre, N° 100 Squadron, RFC
St Inglevert, France; January 1918.
(Beardmore 160 hp)

SOPWITH 1½ STRUTTER

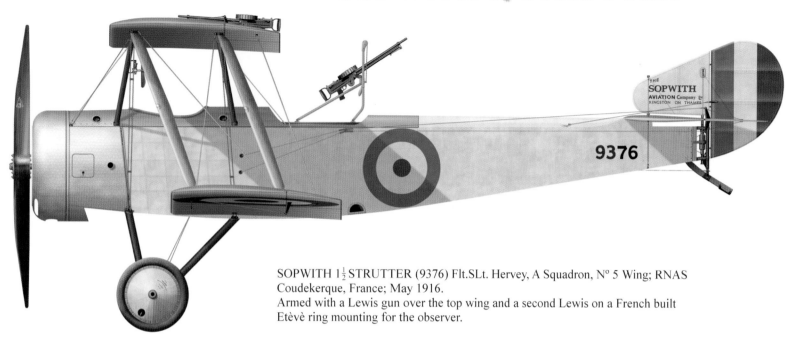

SOPWITH 1½ STRUTTER (9376) Flt.SLt. Hervey, A Squadron, Nº 5 Wing; RNAS Coudekerque, France; May 1916.
Armed with a Lewis gun over the top wing and a second Lewis on a French built Etèvè ring mounting for the observer.

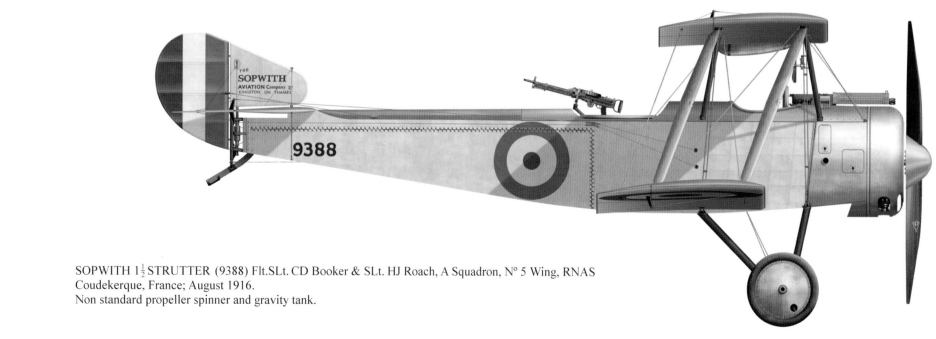

SOPWITH 1½ STRUTTER (9388) Flt.SLt. CD Booker & SLt. HJ Roach, A Squadron, Nº 5 Wing, RNAS Coudekerque, France; August 1916.
Non standard propeller spinner and gravity tank.

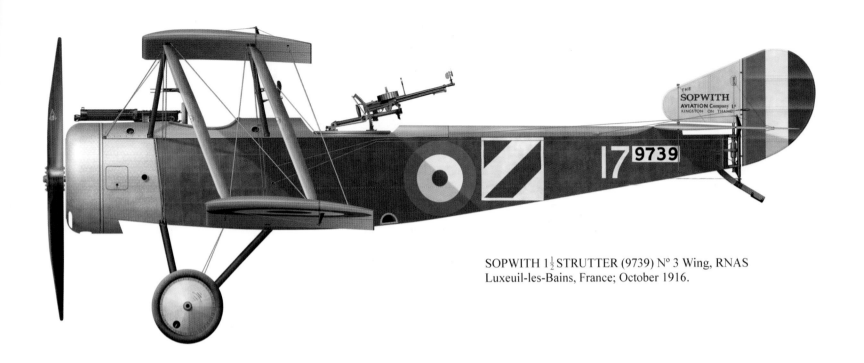

SOPWITH 1½ STRUTTER (9739) Nº 3 Wing, RNAS
Luxeuil-les-Bains, France; October 1916.

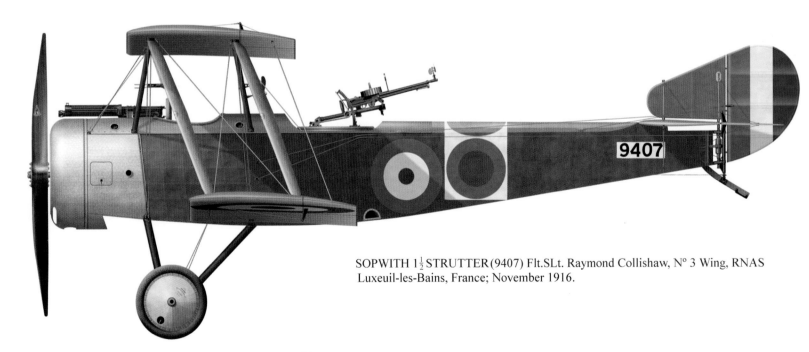

SOPWITH 1½ STRUTTER (9407) Flt.SLt. Raymond Collishaw, Nº 3 Wing, RNAS
Luxeuil-les-Bains, France; November 1916.

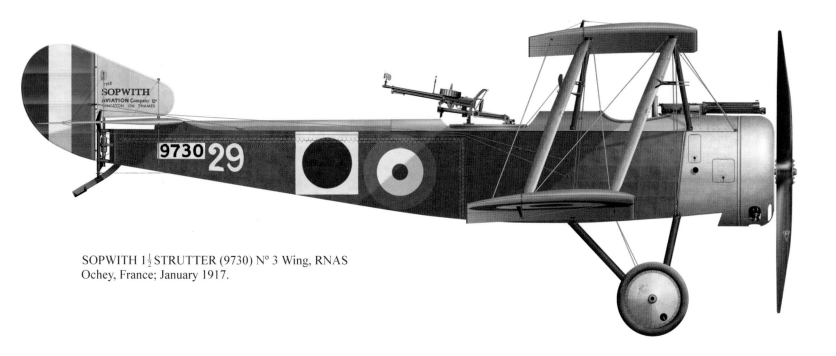

SOPWITH 1½ STRUTTER (9730) Nº 3 Wing, RNAS
Ochey, France; January 1917.

SOPWITH 1½ STRUTTER (N5114) Sqn Cdr. ET Newton-Clare & Lt. Warwick-Wright, Nº 5 Wing, RNAS
Berges, France; February 1917.

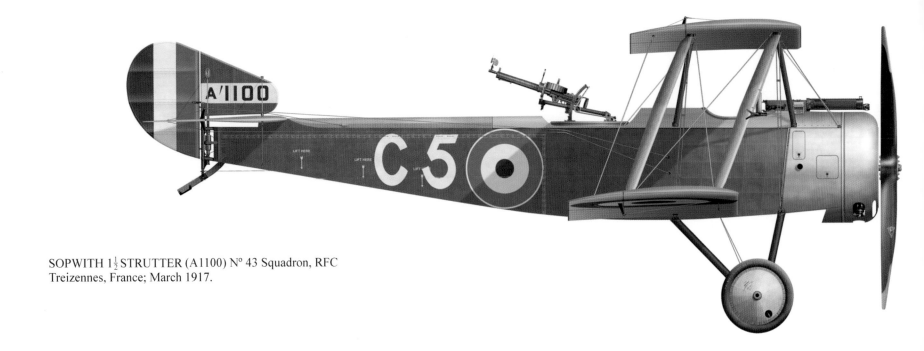

SOPWITH 1½ STRUTTER (A1100) Nº 43 Squadron, RFC
Treizennes, France; March 1917.

SOPWITH 1½ STRUTTER (N5241) 6ᵉᵐᵉ Escadrille, Aviation Militaire Belge
Houtem, Belgium; March 1917.

SOPWITH 1½ STRUTTER (A8337) Nº 43 Squadron, RFC
Treizennes, France; Spring 1917.

SOPWITH 1½ STRUTTER (A993) 2Lt. CM Reece & 2AM A Moult, Nº 43 Squadron, RFC
Treizennes, France; April 1917.

SOPWITH 1½ STRUTTER (A995) Lt. JH Gotch & 2Lt. Kibutz, Nº 70 Squadron, RFC
Estrée Blanche, France; April 1917.

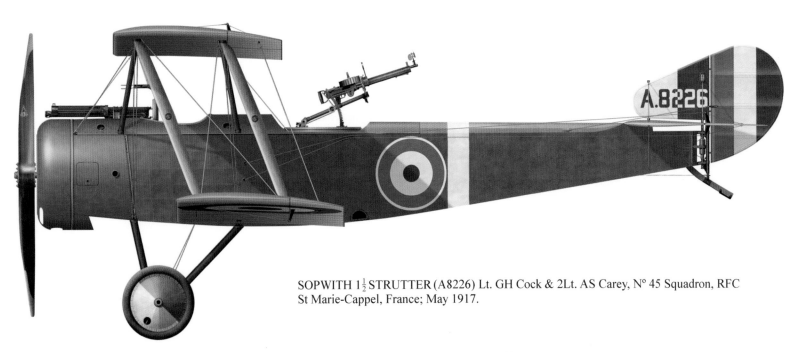

SOPWITH 1½ STRUTTER (A8226) Lt. GH Cock & 2Lt. AS Carey, Nº 45 Squadron, RFC
St Marie-Cappel, France; May 1917.

SOPWITH 1½ STRUTTER (A981) Lt. AS Bourinot & Cpl. A Giles, Nº 70 Squadron, RFC
Liettres, France; June 1917.

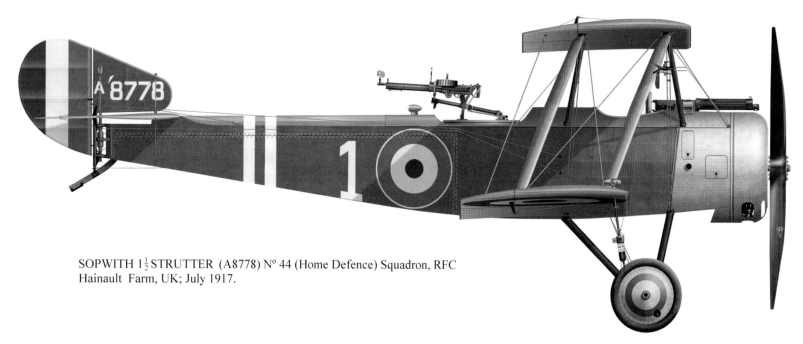

SOPWITH 1½ STRUTTER (A8778) Nº 44 (Home Defence) Squadron, RFC
Hainault Farm, UK; July 1917.

SOPWITH 1½ STRUTTER (B2552) Nº 43 Squadron, RFC
Auchel, France; August 1917.

SOPWITH 1½ STRUTTER (B745) Nº 78 (Home Defence) Squadron, RFC
Sutton's Farm, UK; September 1917.

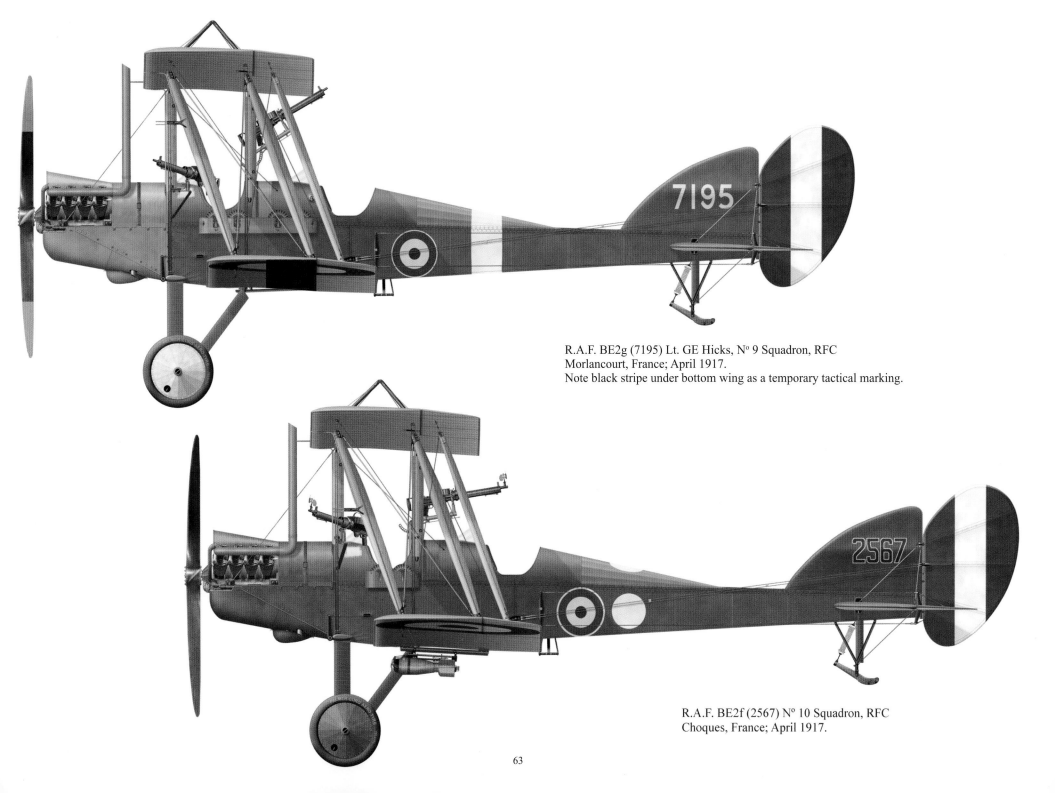

R.A.F. BE2g (7195) Lt. GE Hicks, Nº 9 Squadron, RFC
Morlancourt, France; April 1917.
Note black stripe under bottom wing as a temporary tactical marking.

R.A.F. BE2f (2567) Nº 10 Squadron, RFC
Choques, France; April 1917.

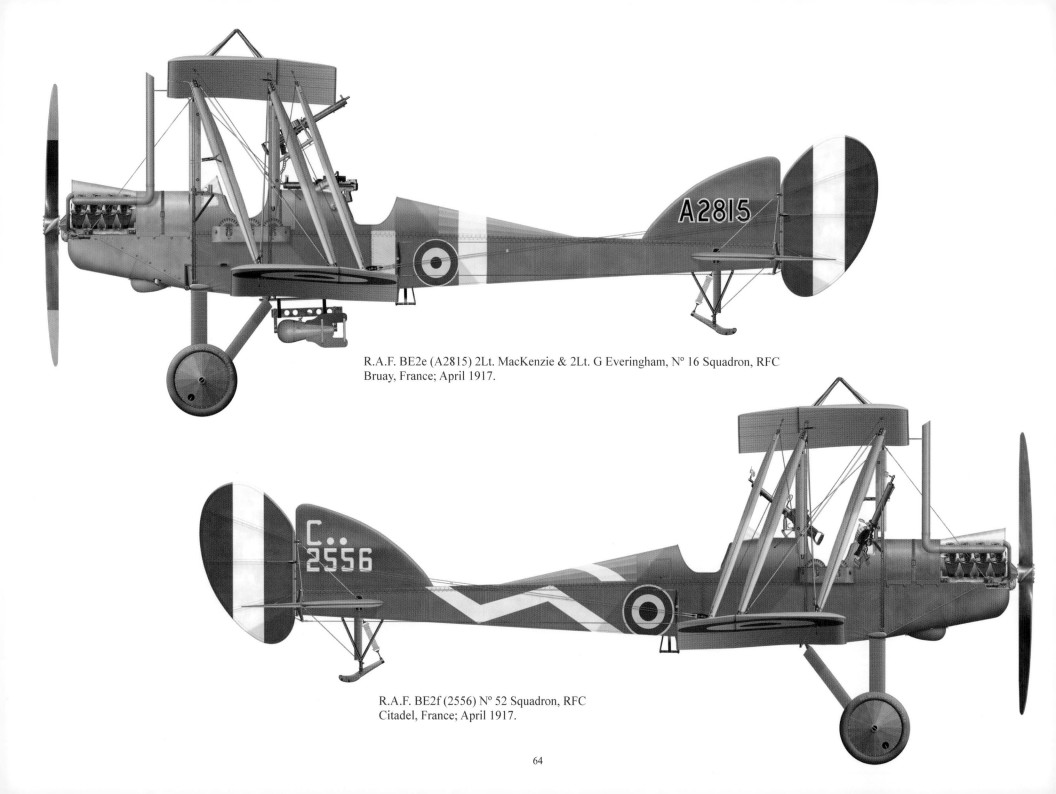

R.A.F. BE2e (A2815) 2Lt. MacKenzie & 2Lt. G Everingham, N° 16 Squadron, RFC
Bruay, France; April 1917.

R.A.F. BE2f (2556) N° 52 Squadron, RFC
Citadel, France; April 1917.

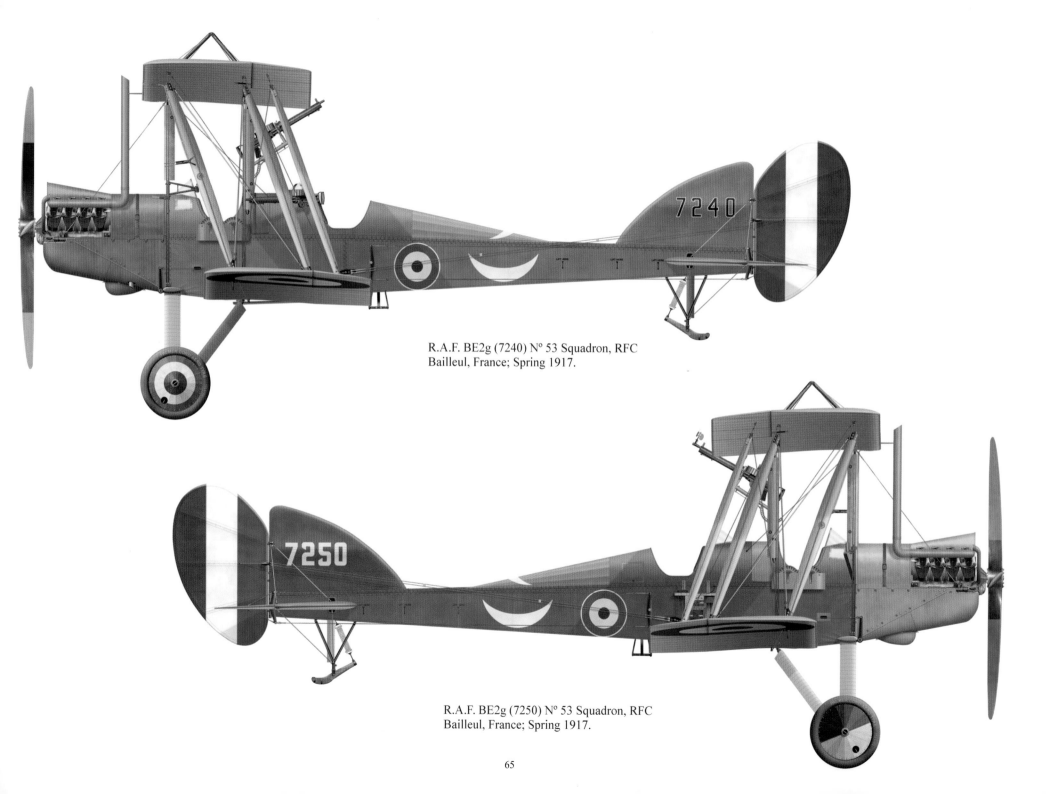

R.A.F. BE2g (7240) Nº 53 Squadron, RFC
Bailleul, France; Spring 1917.

R.A.F. BE2g (7250) Nº 53 Squadron, RFC
Bailleul, France; Spring 1917.

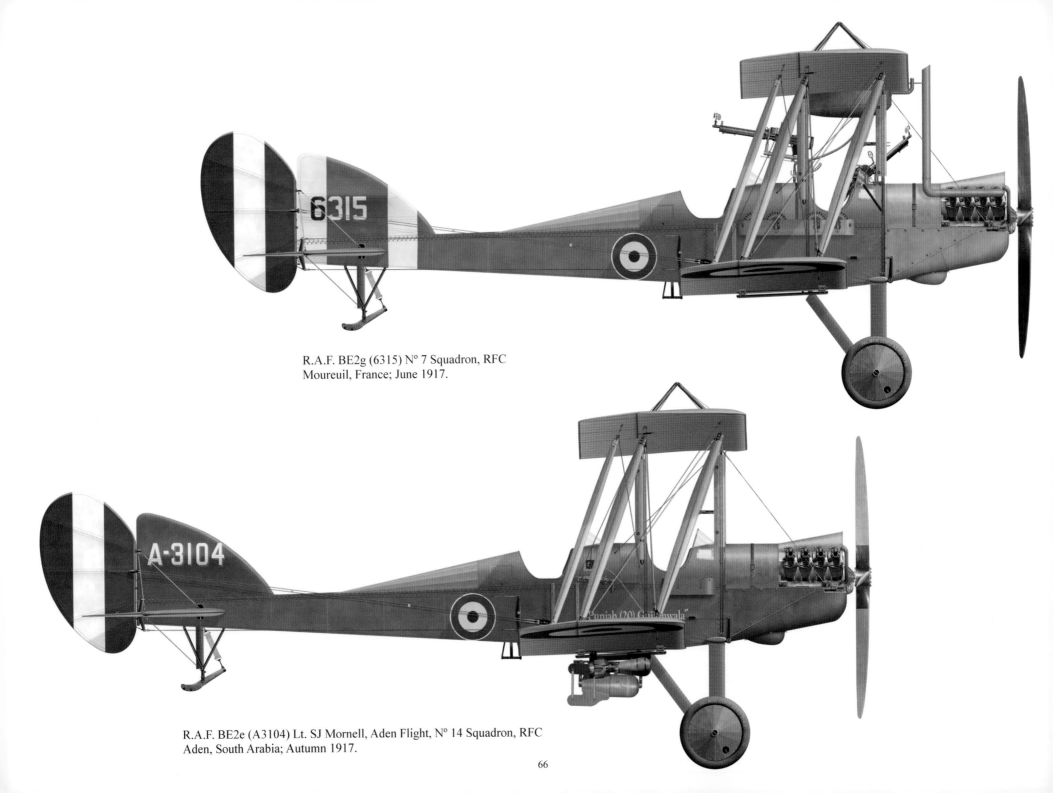

R.A.F. BE2g (6315) N° 7 Squadron, RFC
Moureuil, France; June 1917.

R.A.F. BE2e (A3104) Lt. SJ Mornell, Aden Flight, N° 14 Squadron, RFC
Aden, South Arabia; Autumn 1917.

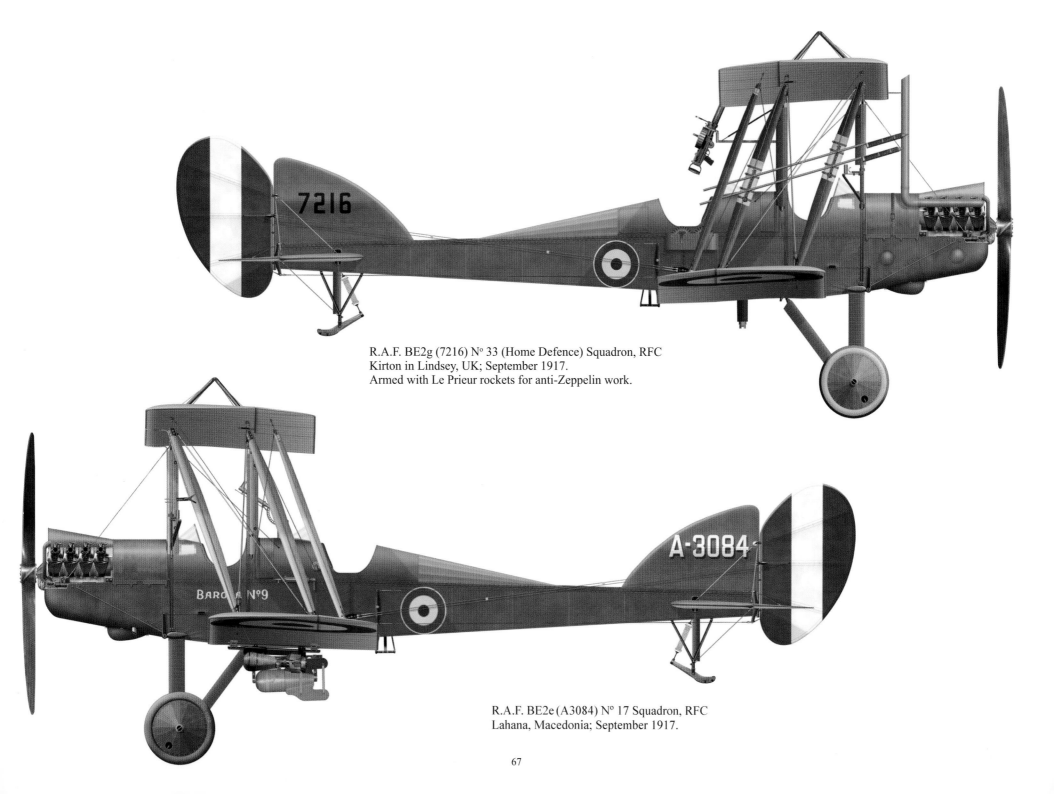

R.A.F. BE2g (7216) Nº 33 (Home Defence) Squadron, RFC
Kirton in Lindsey, UK; September 1917.
Armed with Le Prieur rockets for anti-Zeppelin work.

R.A.F. BE2e (A3084) Nº 17 Squadron, RFC
Lahana, Macedonia; September 1917.

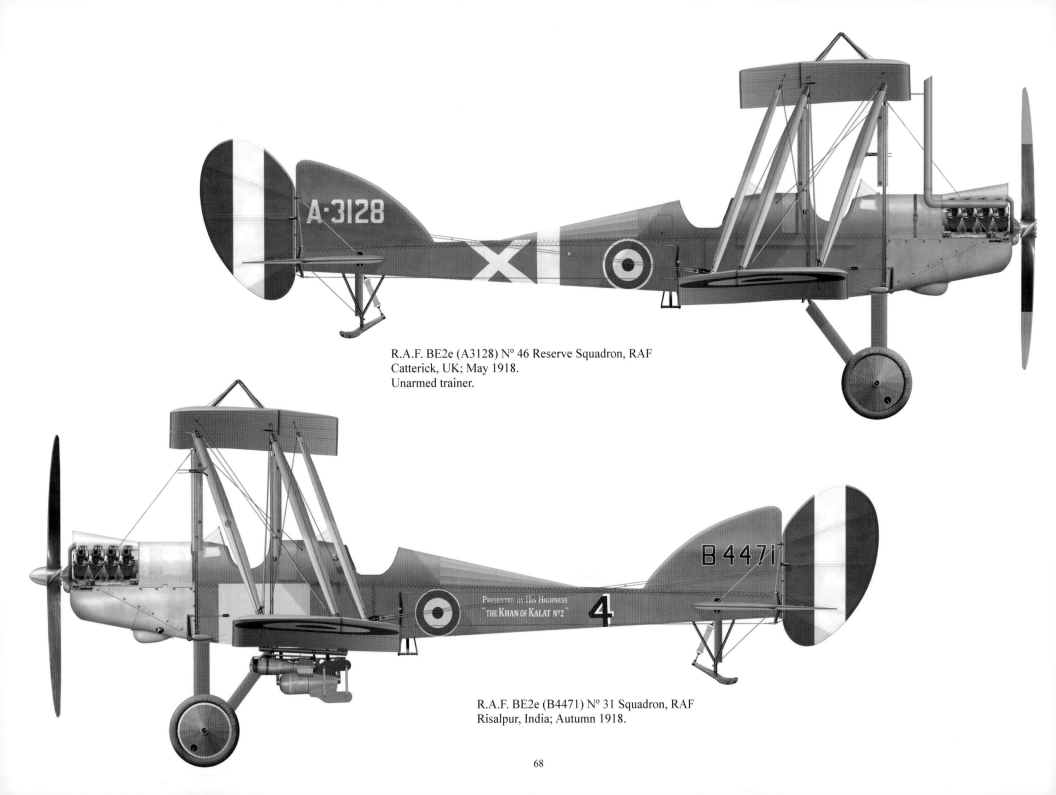

R.A.F. BE2e (A3128) Nº 46 Reserve Squadron, RAF
Catterick, UK; May 1918.
Unarmed trainer.

R.A.F. BE2e (B4471) Nº 31 Squadron, RAF
Risalpur, India; Autumn 1918.

R.A.F. FE2d

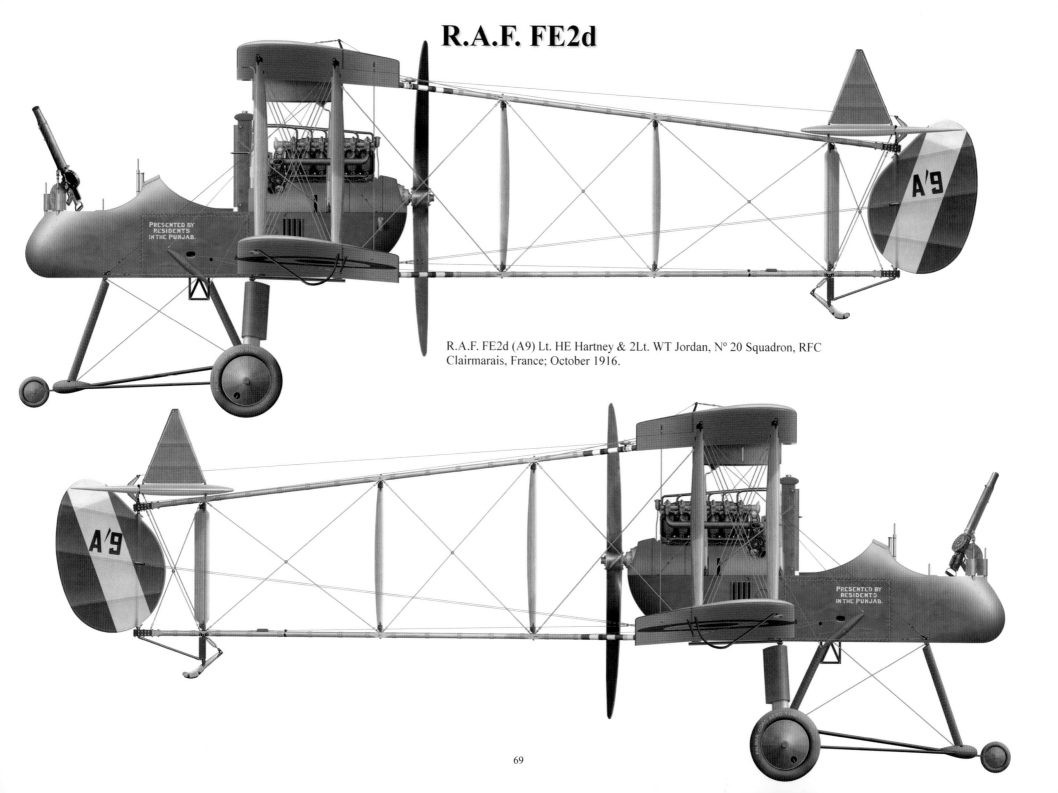

R.A.F. FE2d (A9) Lt. HE Hartney & 2Lt. WT Jordan, N° 20 Squadron, RFC
Clairmarais, France; October 1916.

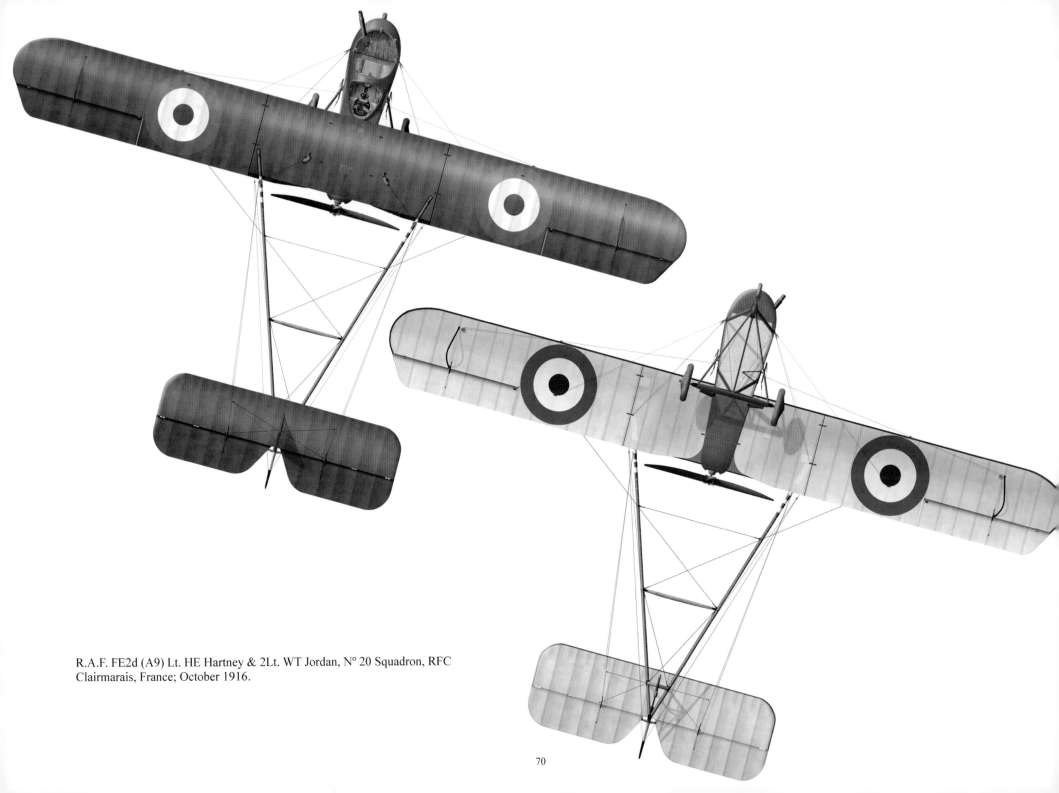

R.A.F. FE2d (A9) Lt. HE Hartney & 2Lt. WT Jordan, Nº 20 Squadron, RFC
Clairmarais, France; October 1916.

70

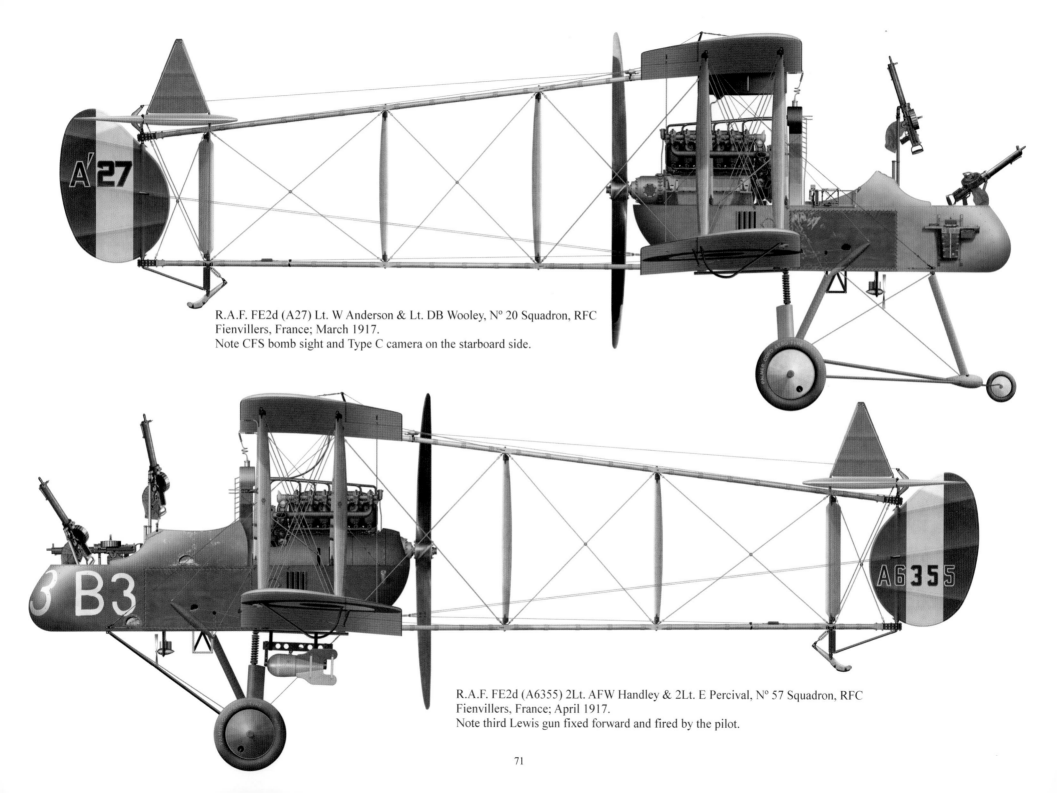

R.A.F. FE2d (A27) Lt. W Anderson & Lt. DB Wooley, Nº 20 Squadron, RFC
Fienvillers, France; March 1917.
Note CFS bomb sight and Type C camera on the starboard side.

R.A.F. FE2d (A6355) 2Lt. AFW Handley & 2Lt. E Percival, Nº 57 Squadron, RFC
Fienvillers, France; April 1917.
Note third Lewis gun fixed forward and fired by the pilot.

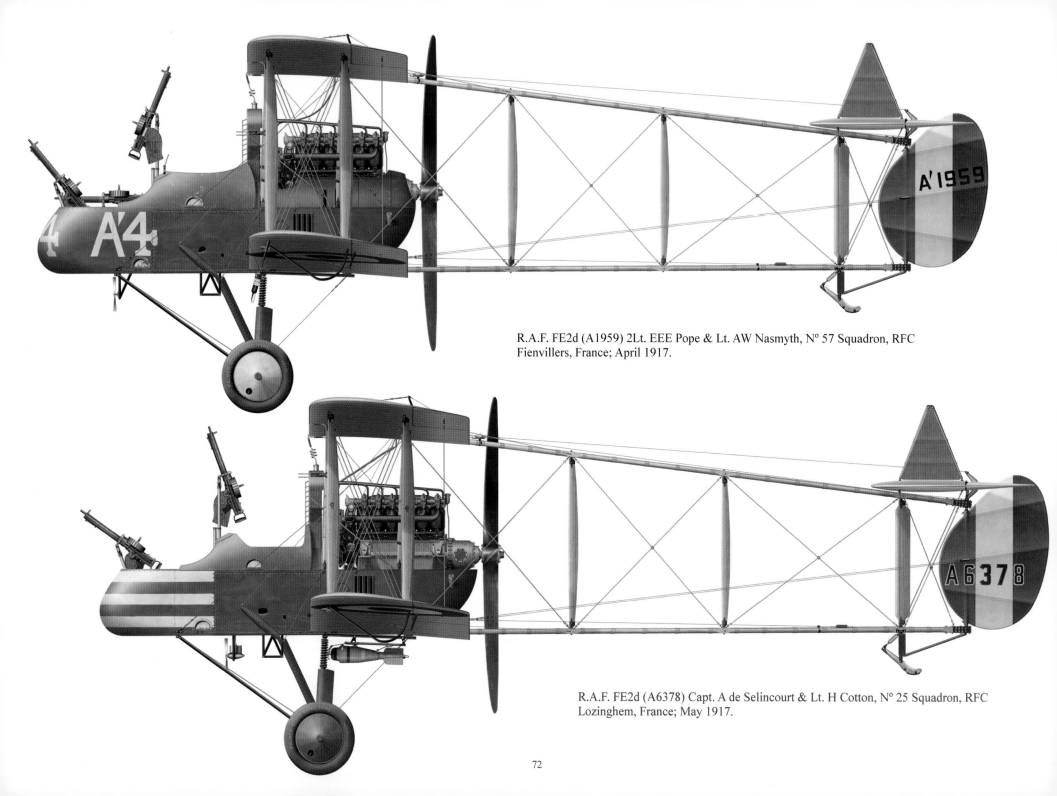

R.A.F. FE2d (A1959) 2Lt. EEE Pope & Lt. AW Nasmyth, Nº 57 Squadron, RFC
Fienvillers, France; April 1917.

R.A.F. FE2d (A6378) Capt. A de Selincourt & Lt. H Cotton, Nº 25 Squadron, RFC
Lozinghem, France; May 1917.

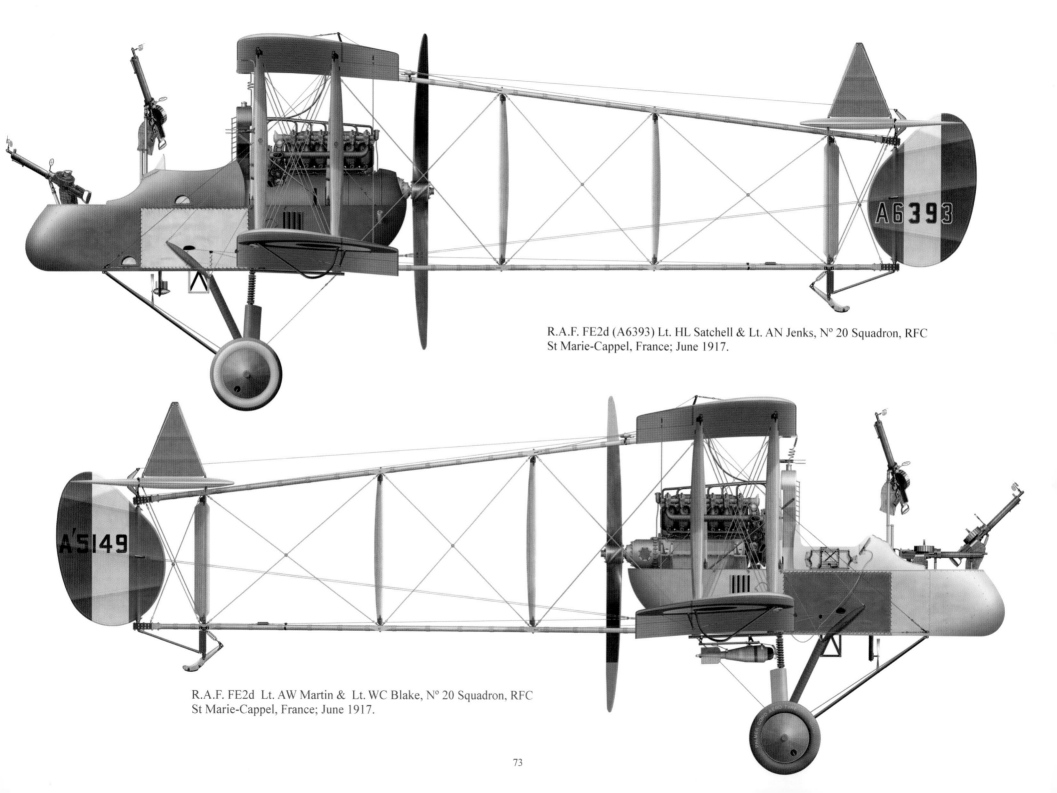

R.A.F. FE2d (A6393) Lt. HL Satchell & Lt. AN Jenks, N° 20 Squadron, RFC
St Marie-Cappel, France; June 1917.

R.A.F. FE2d Lt. AW Martin & Lt. WC Blake, N° 20 Squadron, RFC
St Marie-Cappel, France; June 1917.

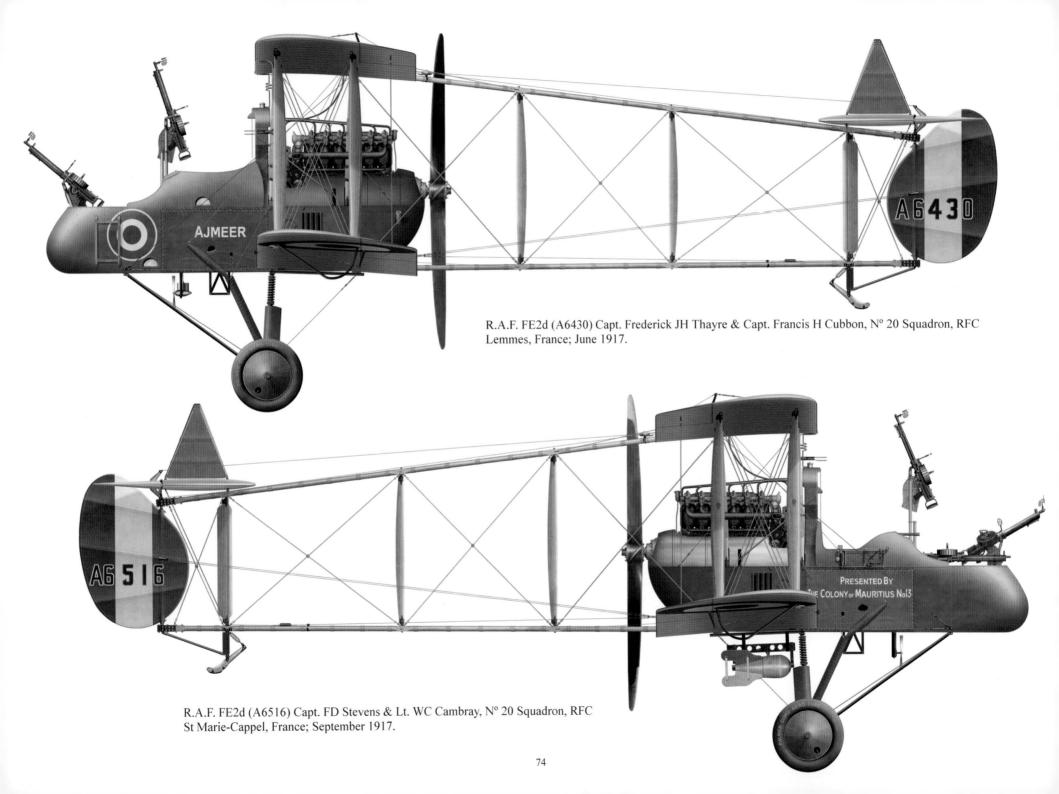

R.A.F. FE2d (A6430) Capt. Frederick JH Thayre & Capt. Francis H Cubbon, Nº 20 Squadron, RFC
Lemmes, France; June 1917.

R.A.F. FE2d (A6516) Capt. FD Stevens & Lt. WC Cambray, Nº 20 Squadron, RFC
St Marie-Cappel, France; September 1917.

ARMSTRONG WHITWORTH FK8

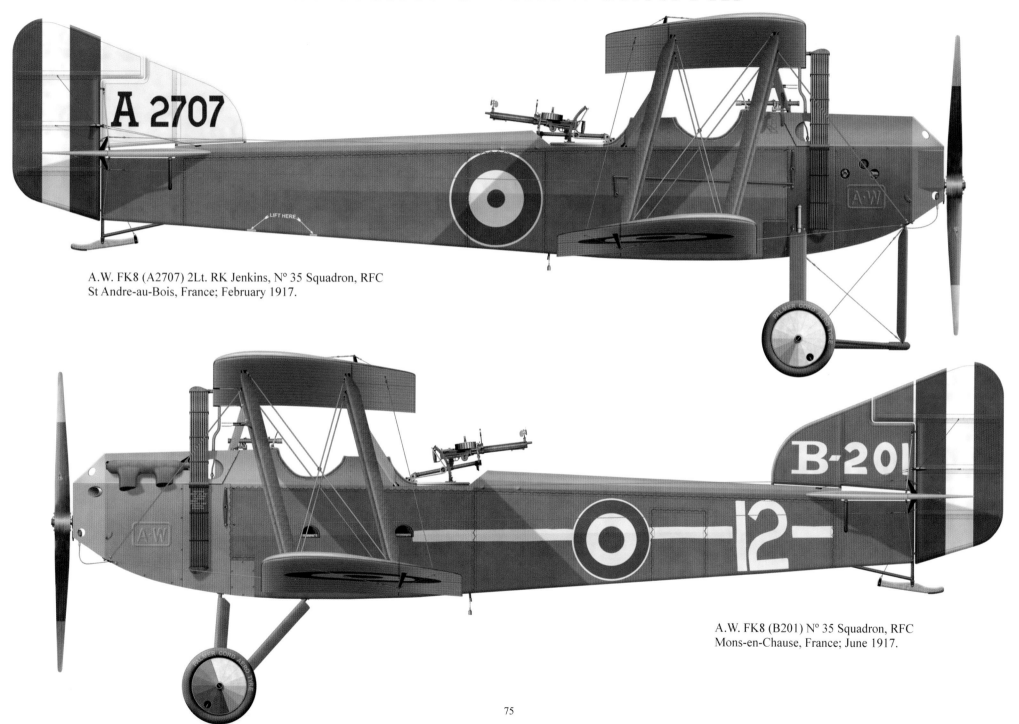

A.W. FK8 (A2707) 2Lt. RK Jenkins, Nº 35 Squadron, RFC
St Andre-au-Bois, France; February 1917.

A.W. FK8 (B201) Nº 35 Squadron, RFC
Mons-en-Chause, France; June 1917.

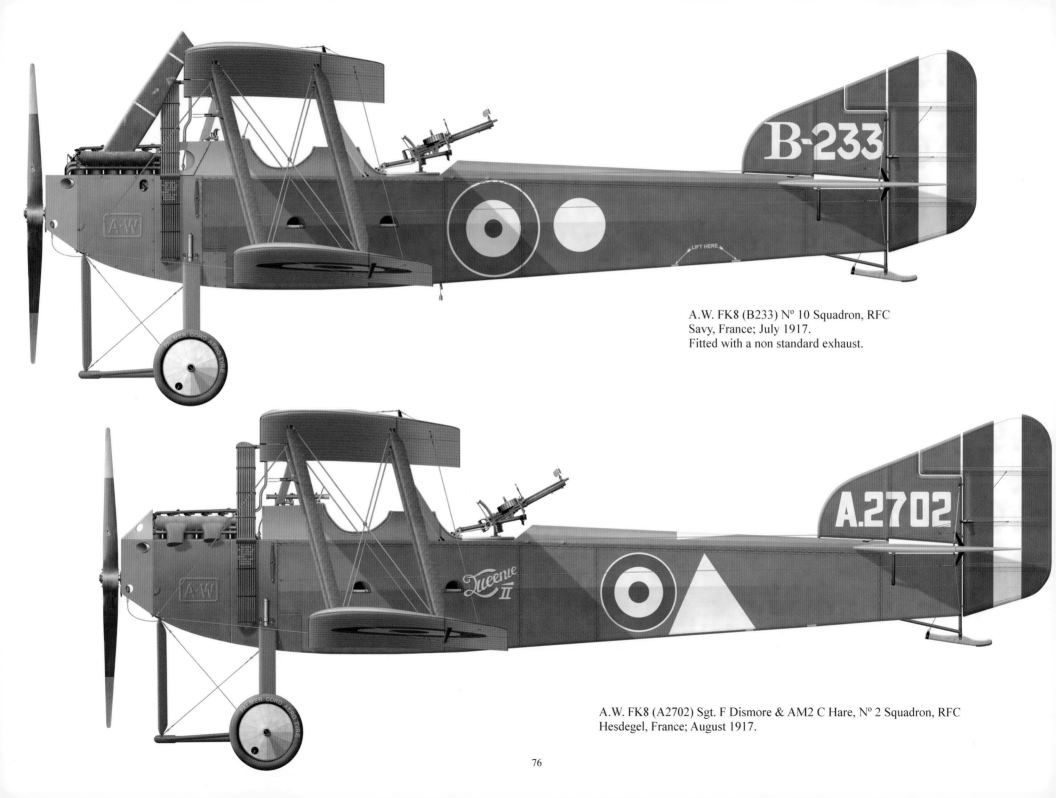

A.W. FK8 (B233) Nº 10 Squadron, RFC
Savy, France; July 1917.
Fitted with a non standard exhaust.

A.W. FK8 (A2702) Sgt. F Dismore & AM2 C Hare, Nº 2 Squadron, RFC
Hesdegel, France; August 1917.

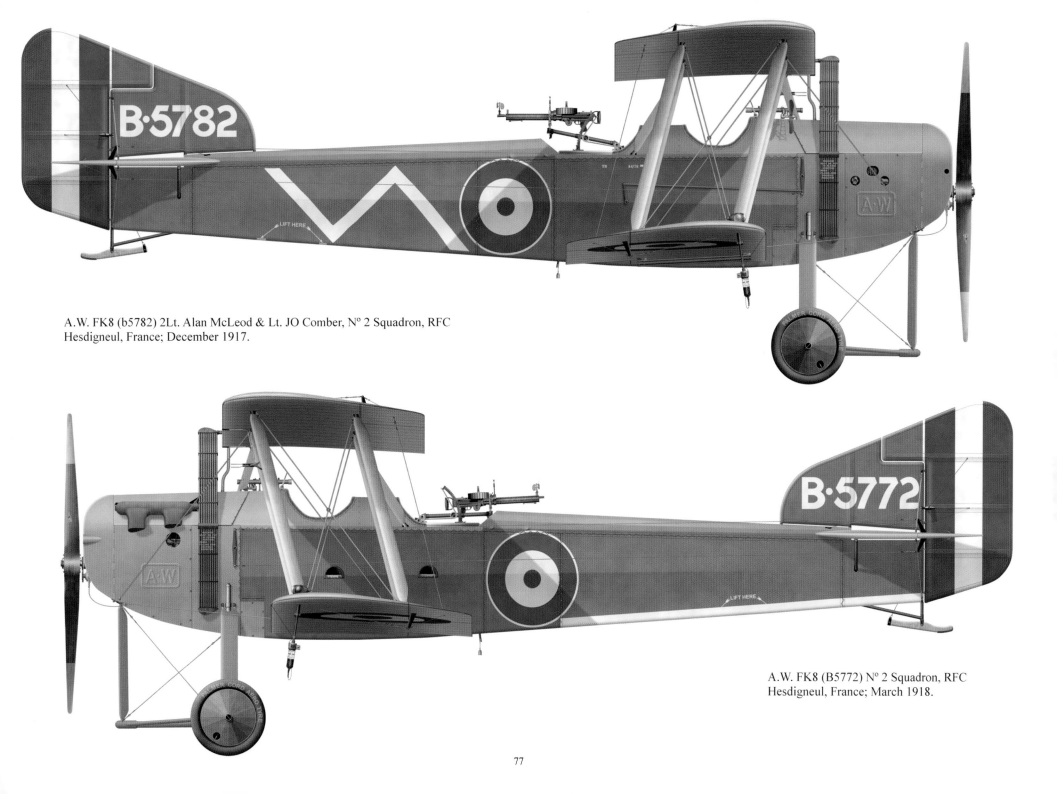

A.W. FK8 (b5782) 2Lt. Alan McLeod & Lt. JO Comber, N° 2 Squadron, RFC
Hesdigneul, France; December 1917.

A.W. FK8 (B5772) N° 2 Squadron, RFC
Hesdigneul, France; March 1918.

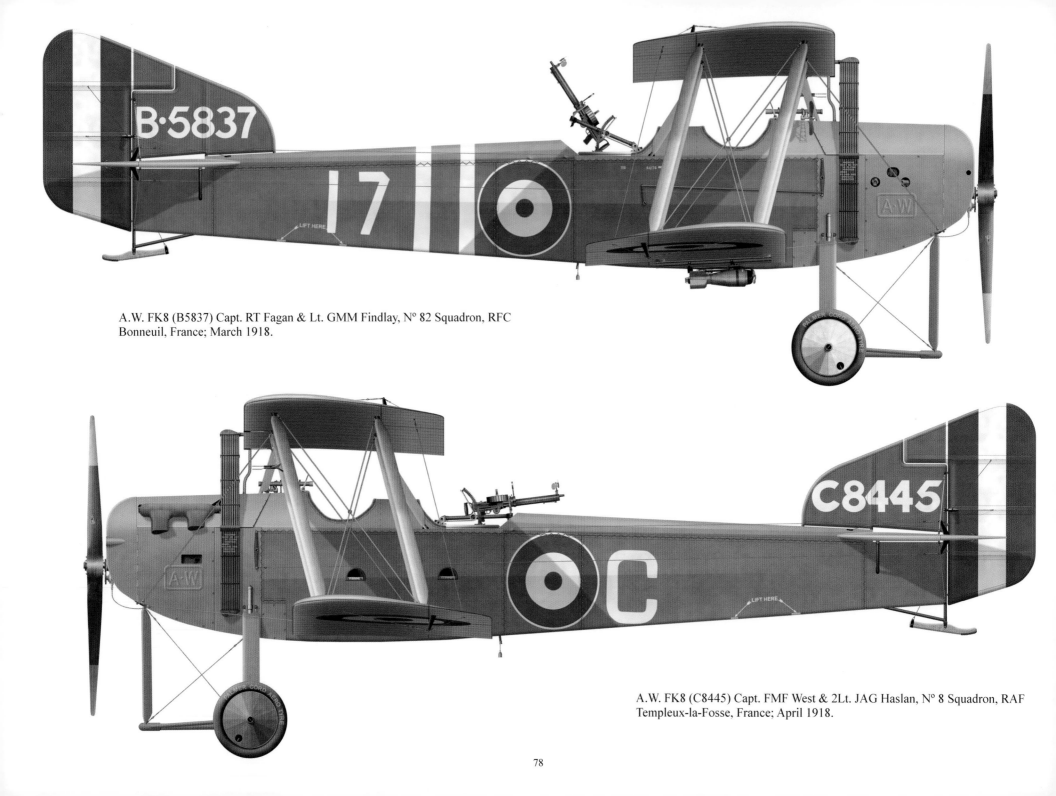

A.W. FK8 (B5837) Capt. RT Fagan & Lt. GMM Findlay, Nº 82 Squadron, RFC
Bonneuil, France; March 1918.

A.W. FK8 (C8445) Capt. FMF West & 2Lt. JAG Haslan, Nº 8 Squadron, RAF
Templeux-la-Fosse, France; April 1918.

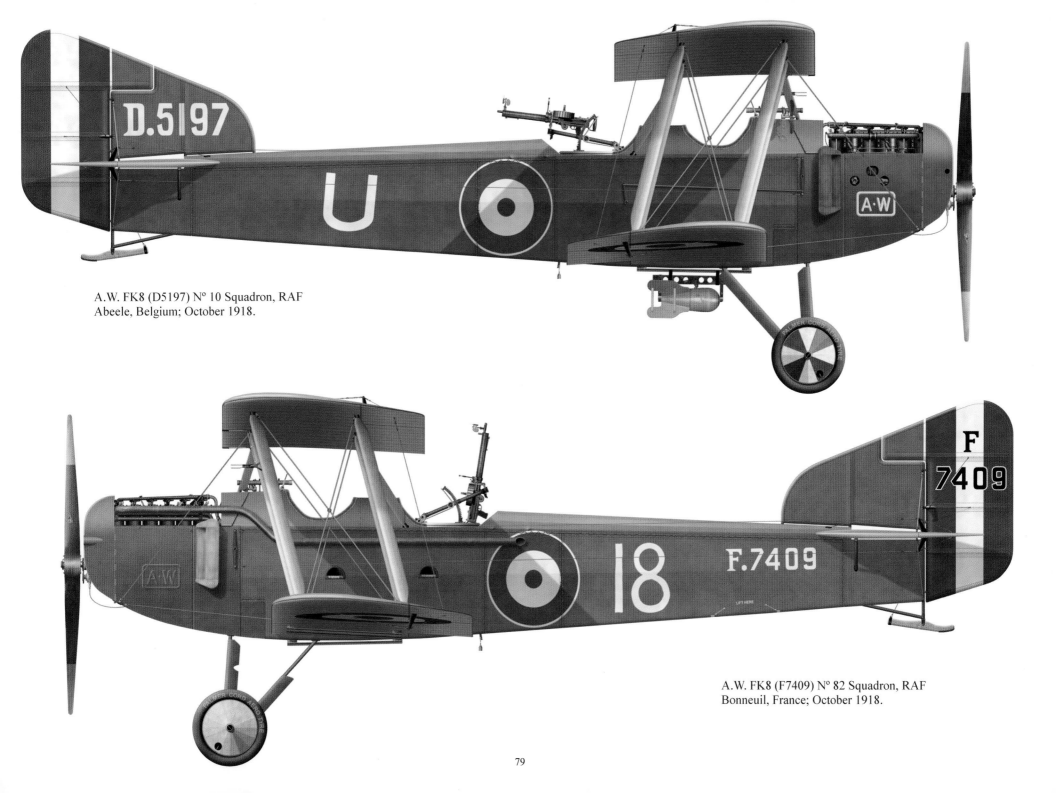

A.W. FK8 (D5197) Nº 10 Squadron, RAF
Abeele, Belgium; October 1918.

A.W. FK8 (F7409) Nº 82 Squadron, RAF
Bonneuil, France; October 1918.

A.M.C. DH4

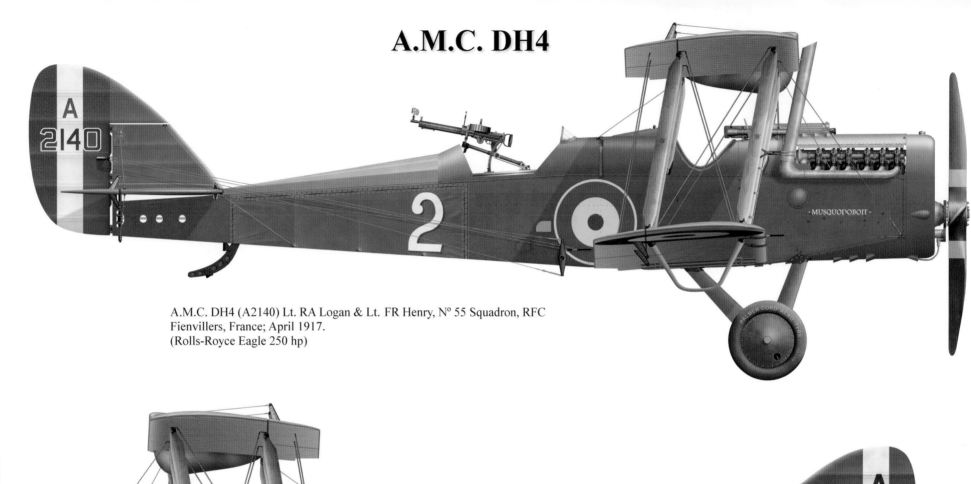

A.M.C. DH4 (A2140) Lt. RA Logan & Lt. FR Henry, Nº 55 Squadron, RFC
Fienvillers, France; April 1917.
(Rolls-Royce Eagle 250 hp)

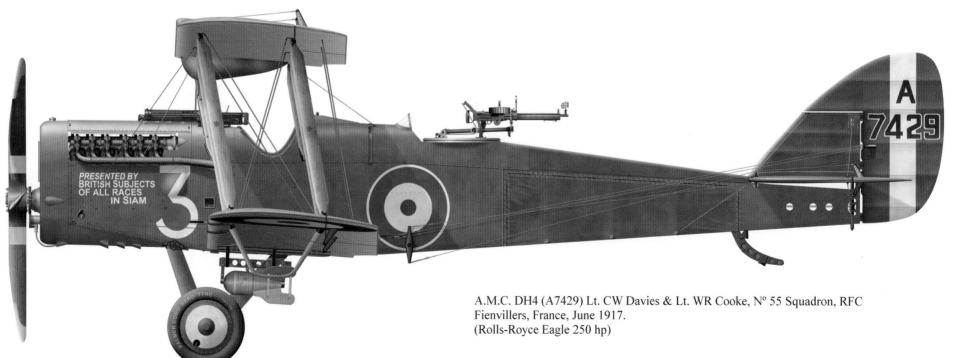

A.M.C. DH4 (A7429) Lt. CW Davies & Lt. WR Cooke, Nº 55 Squadron, RFC
Fienvillers, France, June 1917.
(Rolls-Royce Eagle 250 hp)

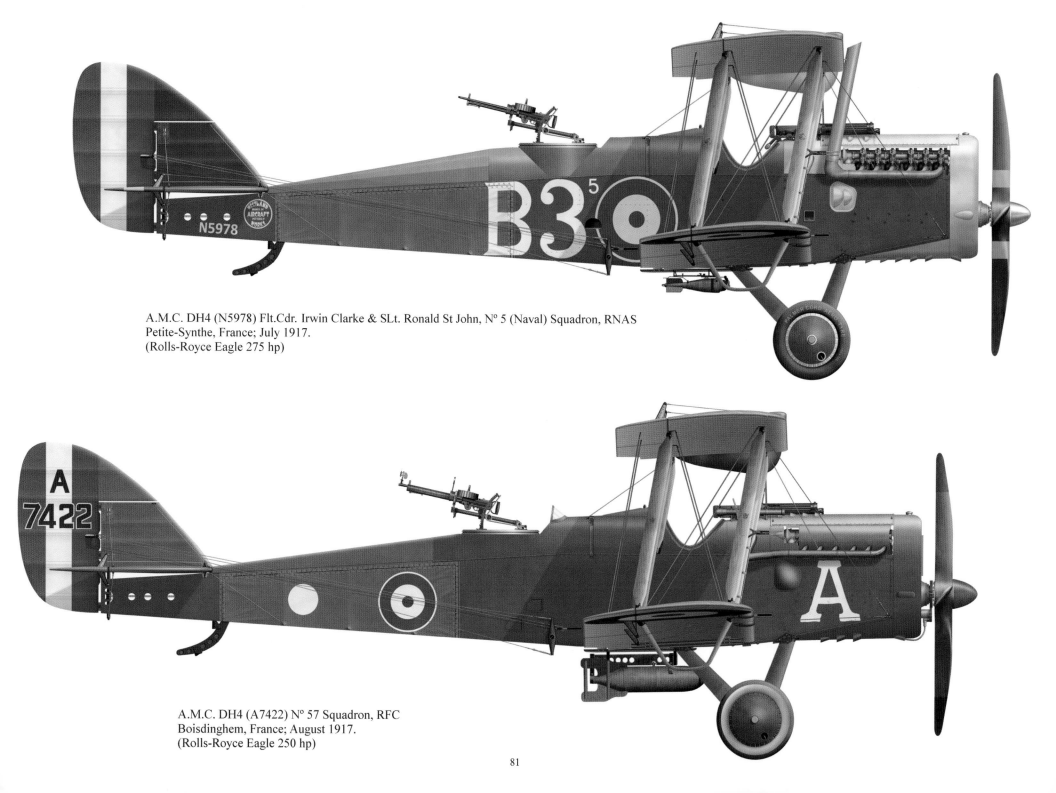

A.M.C. DH4 (N5978) Flt.Cdr. Irwin Clarke & SLt. Ronald St John, Nº 5 (Naval) Squadron, RNAS
Petite-Synthe, France; July 1917.
(Rolls-Royce Eagle 275 hp)

A.M.C. DH4 (A7422) Nº 57 Squadron, RFC
Boisdinghem, France; August 1917.
(Rolls-Royce Eagle 250 hp)

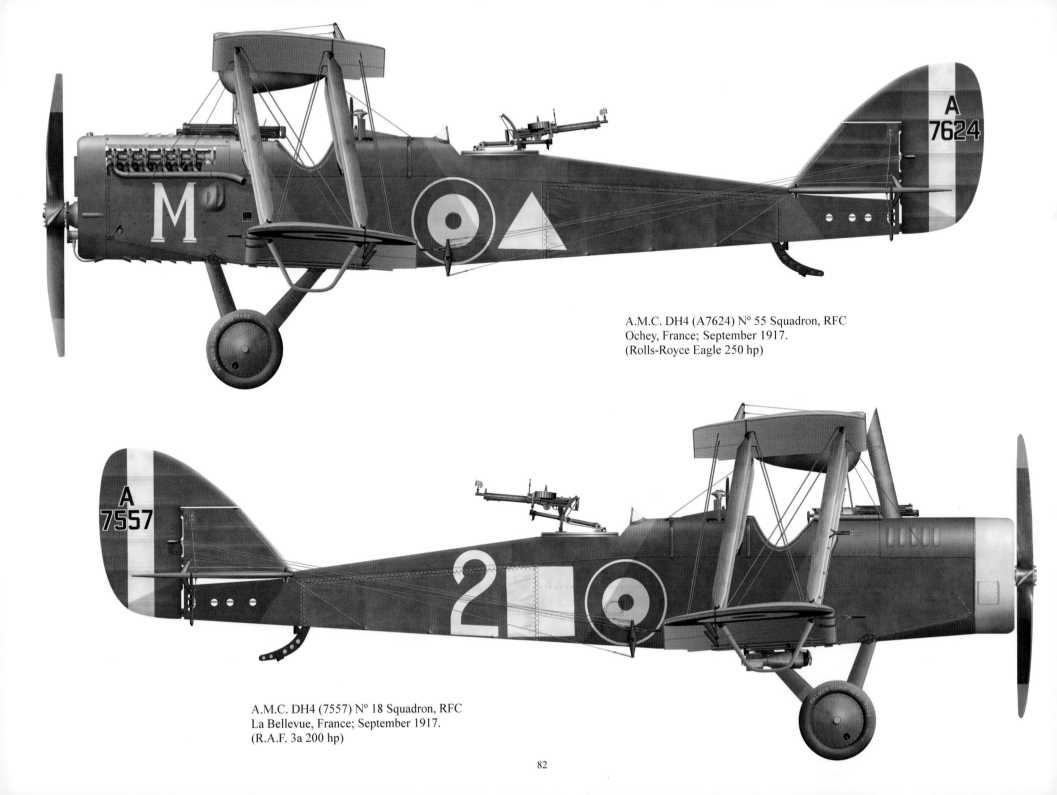

A.M.C. DH4 (A7624) Nº 55 Squadron, RFC
Ochey, France; September 1917.
(Rolls-Royce Eagle 250 hp)

A.M.C. DH4 (7557) Nº 18 Squadron, RFC
La Bellevue, France; September 1917.
(R.A.F. 3a 200 hp)

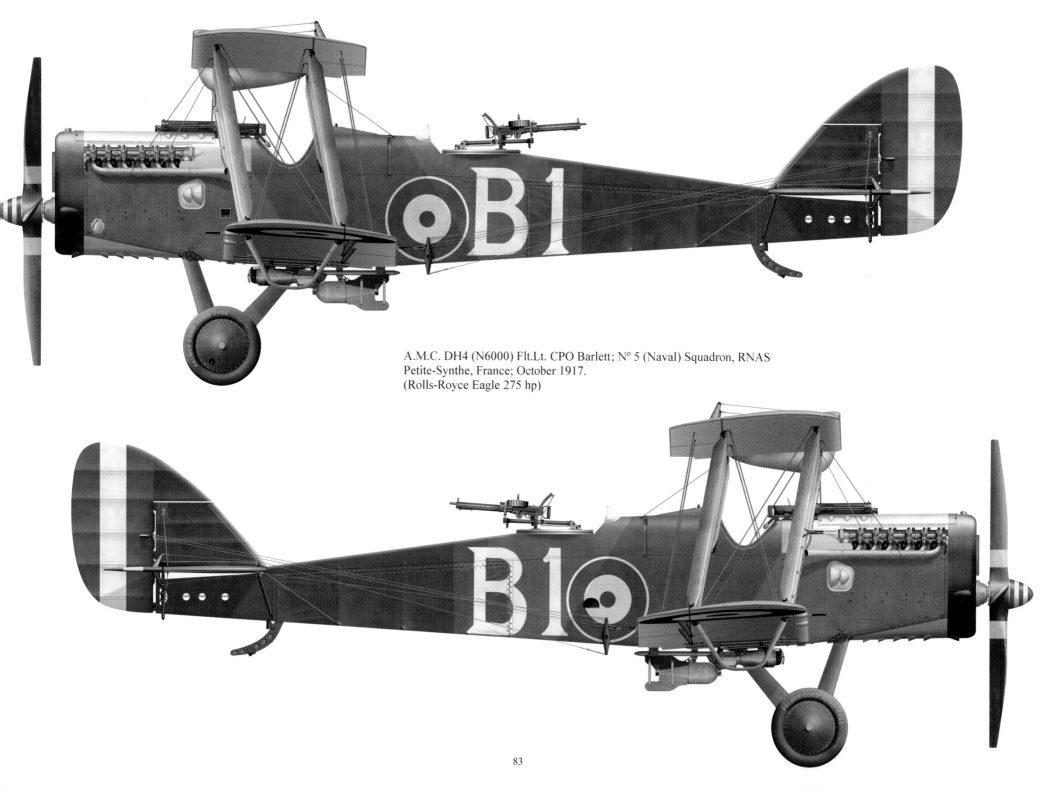

A.M.C. DH4 (N6000) Flt.Lt. CPO Barlett; N° 5 (Naval) Squadron, RNAS
Petite-Synthe, France; October 1917.
(Rolls-Royce Eagle 275 hp)

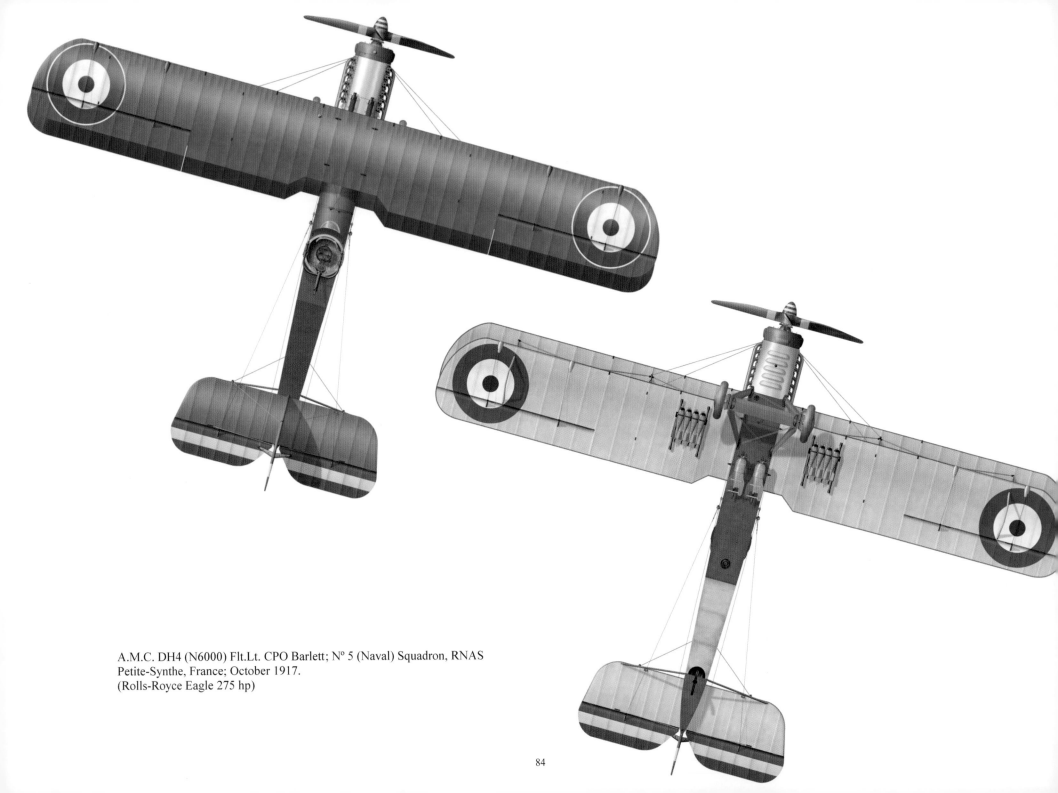

A.M.C. DH4 (N6000) Flt.Lt. CPO Barlett; Nº 5 (Naval) Squadron, RNAS
Petite-Synthe, France; October 1917.
(Rolls-Royce Eagle 275 hp)

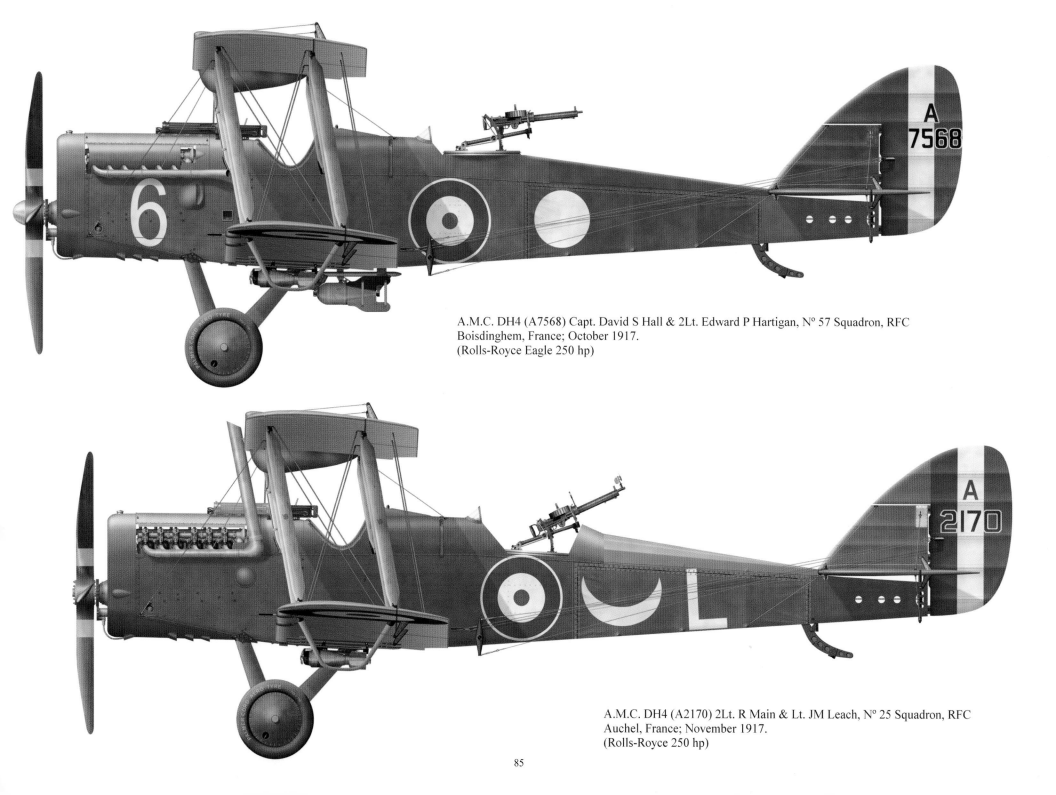

A.M.C. DH4 (A7568) Capt. David S Hall & 2Lt. Edward P Hartigan, Nº 57 Squadron, RFC
Boisdinghem, France; October 1917.
(Rolls-Royce Eagle 250 hp)

A.M.C. DH4 (A2170) 2Lt. R Main & Lt. JM Leach, Nº 25 Squadron, RFC
Auchel, France; November 1917.
(Rolls-Royce 250 hp)

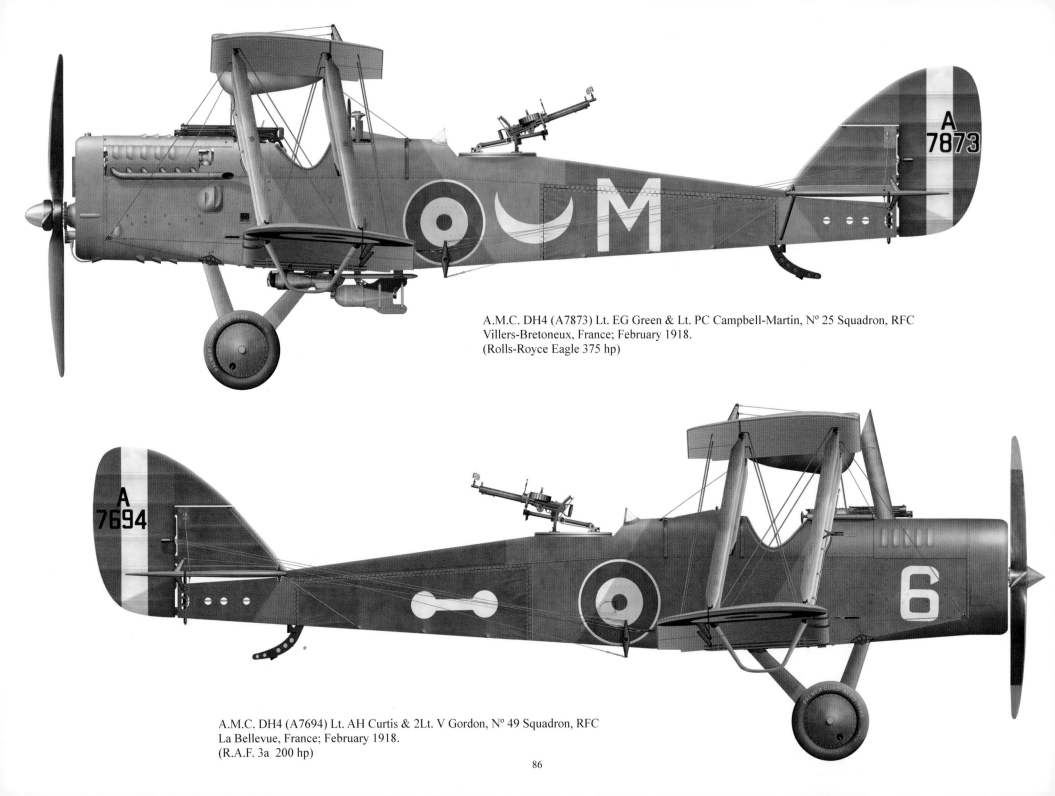

A.M.C. DH4 (A7873) Lt. EG Green & Lt. PC Campbell-Martin, Nº 25 Squadron, RFC
Villers-Bretoneux, France; February 1918.
(Rolls-Royce Eagle 375 hp)

A.M.C. DH4 (A7694) Lt. AH Curtis & 2Lt. V Gordon, Nº 49 Squadron, RFC
La Bellevue, France; February 1918.
(R.A.F. 3a 200 hp)

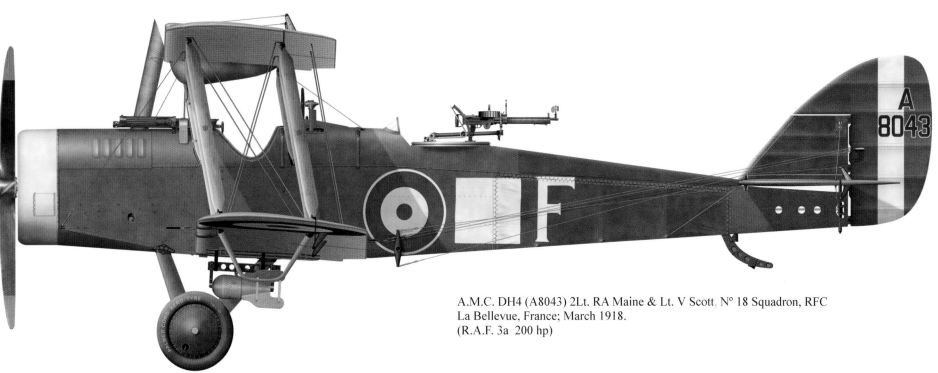

A.M.C. DH4 (A8043) 2Lt. RA Maine & Lt. V Scott, Nº 18 Squadron, RFC
La Bellevue, France; March 1918.
(R.A.F. 3a 200 hp)

A.M.C. DH4 (B3957) Capt. F
Azelot, France; June 1918
(Rolls-Royce Eagle 275 hp)

A.M.C. DH4 (B2071) Nº 27 Squadron, RAF
Ruisseauville, France; April 1918.
(Siddeley Puma 230 hp)

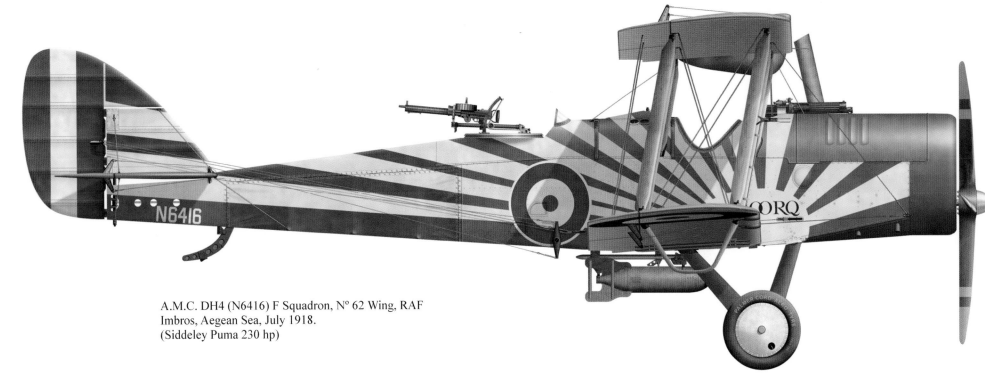

A.M.C.
Berges
Note fa
(Rolls-

A.M.C. DH4 (N6416) F Squadron, N° 62 Wing, RAF
Imbros, Aegean Sea, July 1918.
(Siddeley Puma 230 hp)

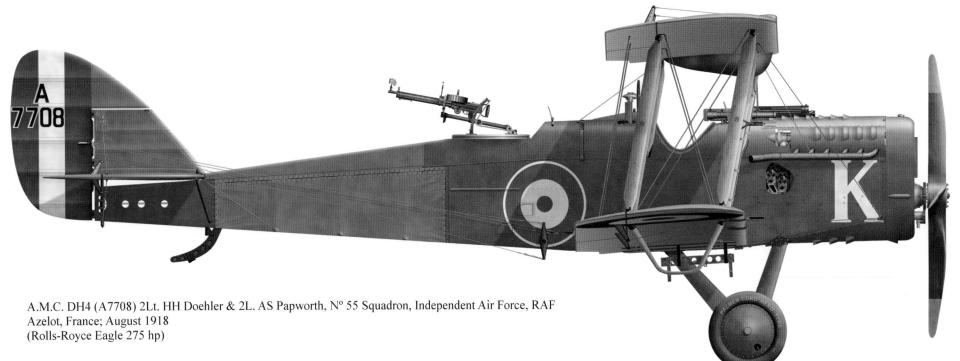

A.M.C. DH4 (A7708) 2Lt. HH Doehler & 2L. AS Papworth, N° 55 Squadron, Independent Air Force, RAF
Azelot, France; August 1918
(Rolls-Royce Eagle 275 hp)

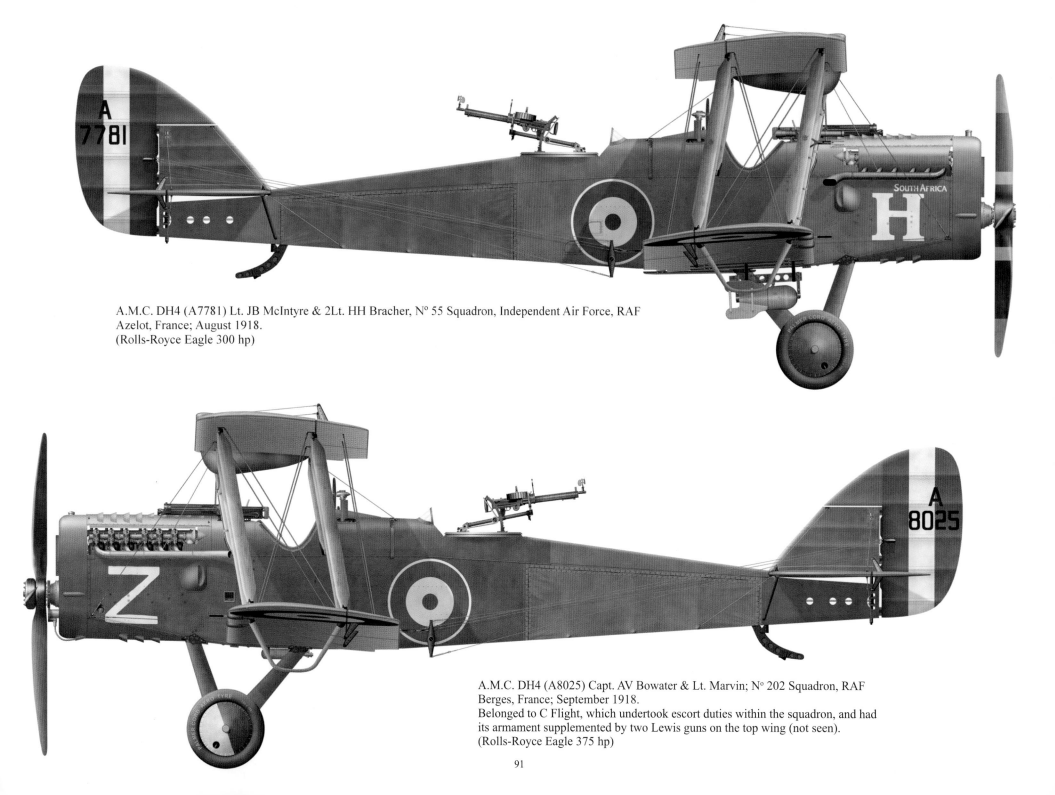

A.M.C. DH4 (A7781) Lt. JB McIntyre & 2Lt. HH Bracher, Nº 55 Squadron, Independent Air Force, RAF
Azelot, France; August 1918.
(Rolls-Royce Eagle 300 hp)

A.M.C. DH4 (A8025) Capt. AV Bowater & Lt. Marvin; Nº 202 Squadron, RAF
Berges, France; September 1918.
Belonged to C Flight, which undertook escort duties within the squadron, and had
its armament supplemented by two Lewis guns on the top wing (not seen).
(Rolls-Royce Eagle 375 hp)

A.M.C. DH4 (N5997) Lt. Robert Coulthard & 2Lt. Leonard Timmis, Nº 202 Squadron, RAF
Berges, France; October 1918.
(Rolls-Royce 375 hp)

A.M.C. DH4 (F5721) Nº 217 Squadron, RAF
Berges, France; November 1918.
(Rolls-Royce 375 hp)

R.A.F. RE8

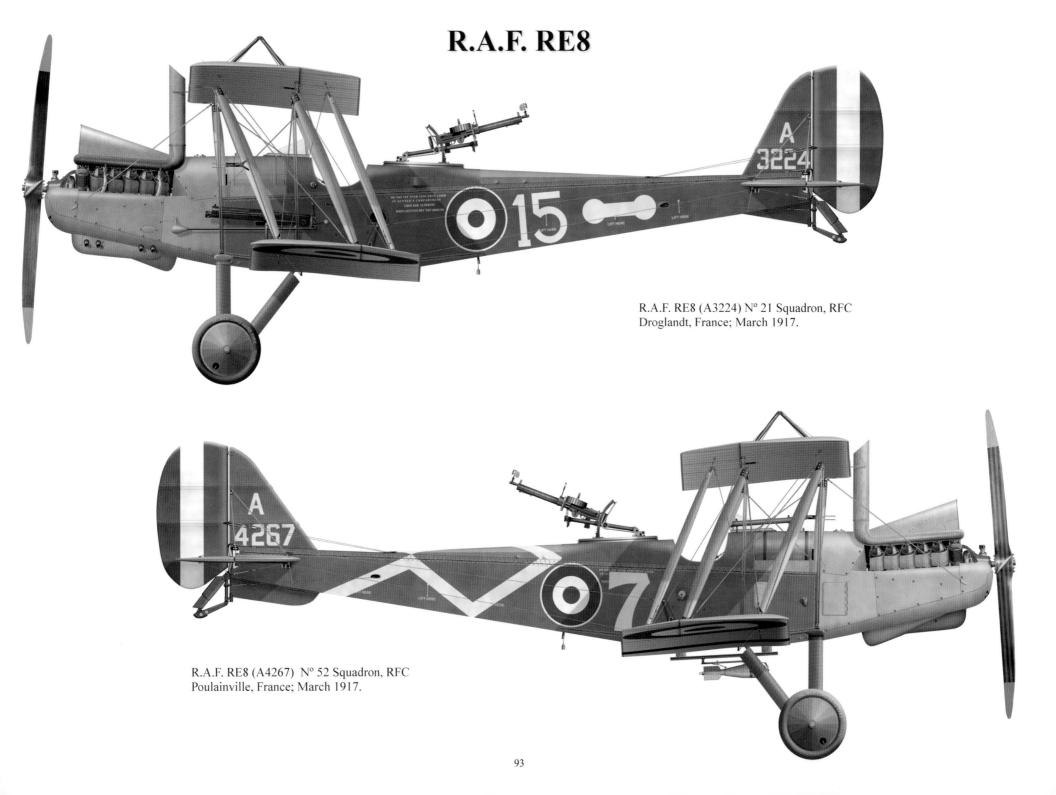

R.A.F. RE8 (A3224) Nº 21 Squadron, RFC
Droglandt, France; March 1917.

R.A.F. RE8 (A4267) Nº 52 Squadron, RFC
Poulainville, France; March 1917.

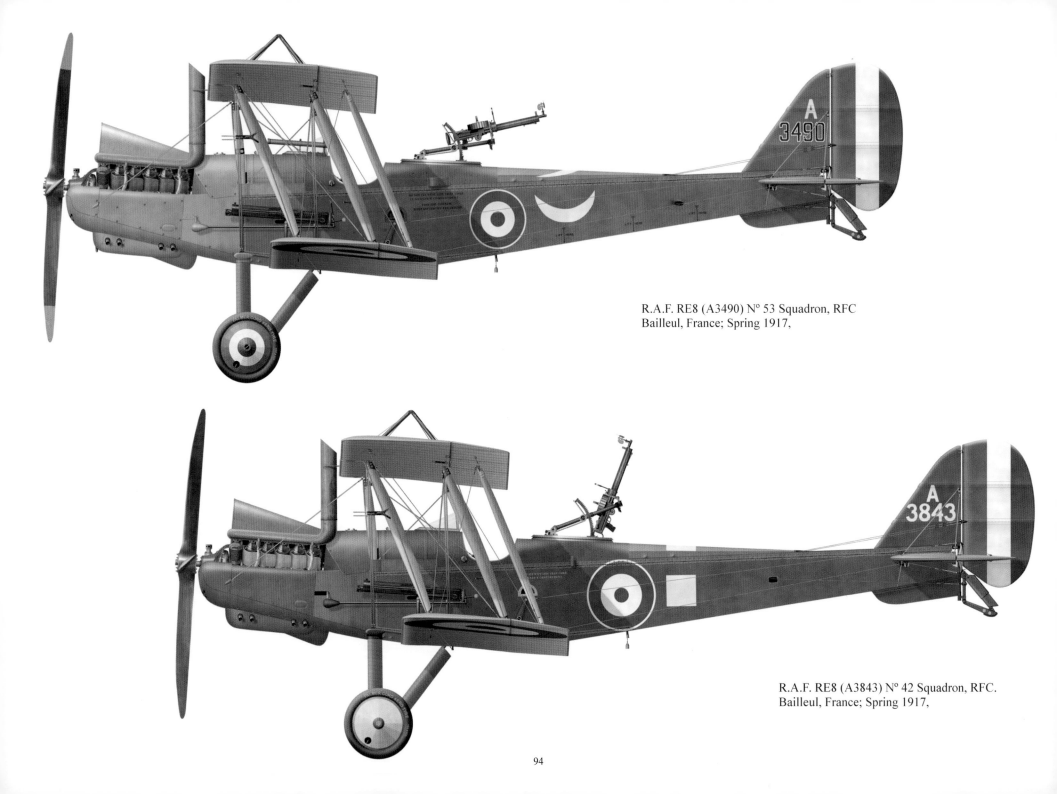

R.A.F. RE8 (A3490) Nº 53 Squadron, RFC
Bailleul, France; Spring 1917,

R.A.F. RE8 (A3843) Nº 42 Squadron, RFC.
Bailleul, France; Spring 1917,

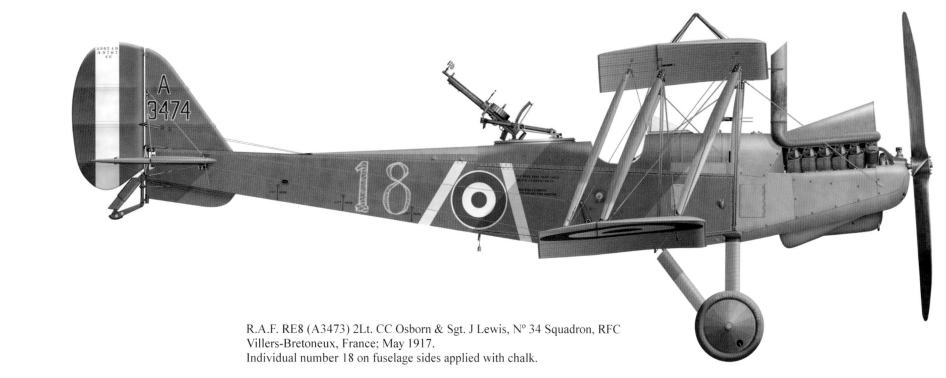

R.A.F. RE8 (A3473) 2Lt. CC Osborn & Sgt. J Lewis, N° 34 Squadron, RFC
Villers-Bretoneux, France; May 1917.
Individual number 18 on fuselage sides applied with chalk.

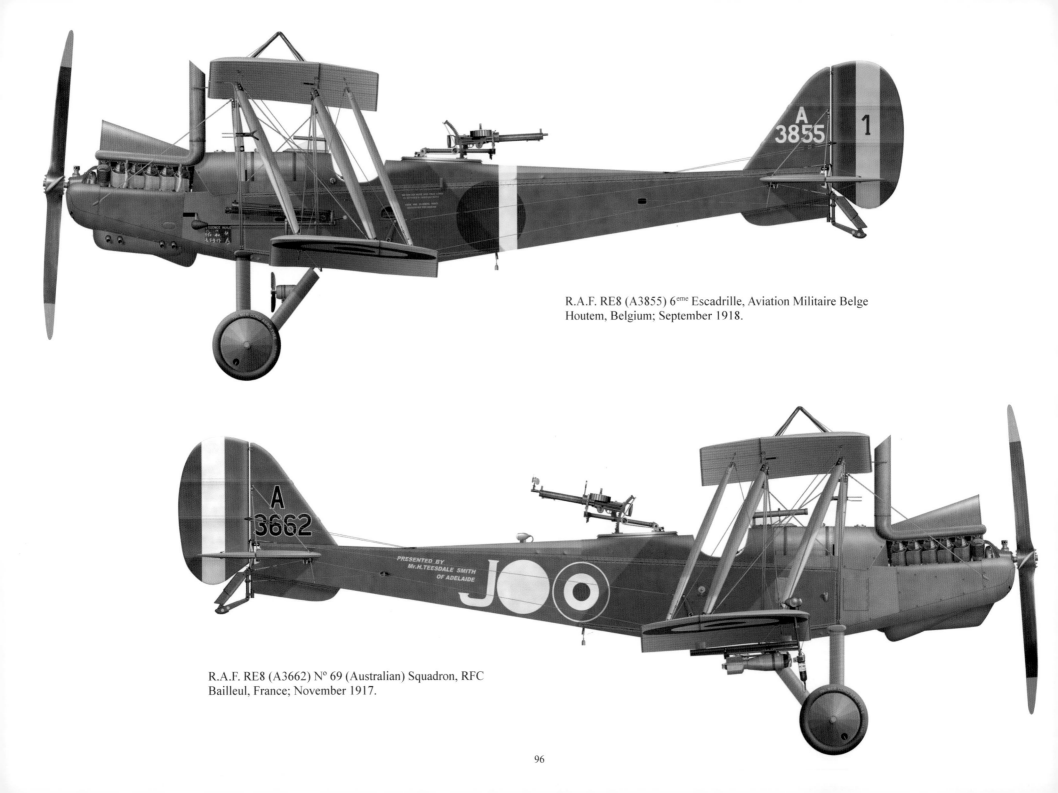

R.A.F. RE8 (A3855) 6eme Escadrille, Aviation Militaire Belge
Houtem, Belgium; September 1918.

R.A.F. RE8 (A3662) N° 69 (Australian) Squadron, RFC
Bailleul, France; November 1917.

PRESENTED BY
Mr.H.TEESDALE SMITH
OF ADELAIDE

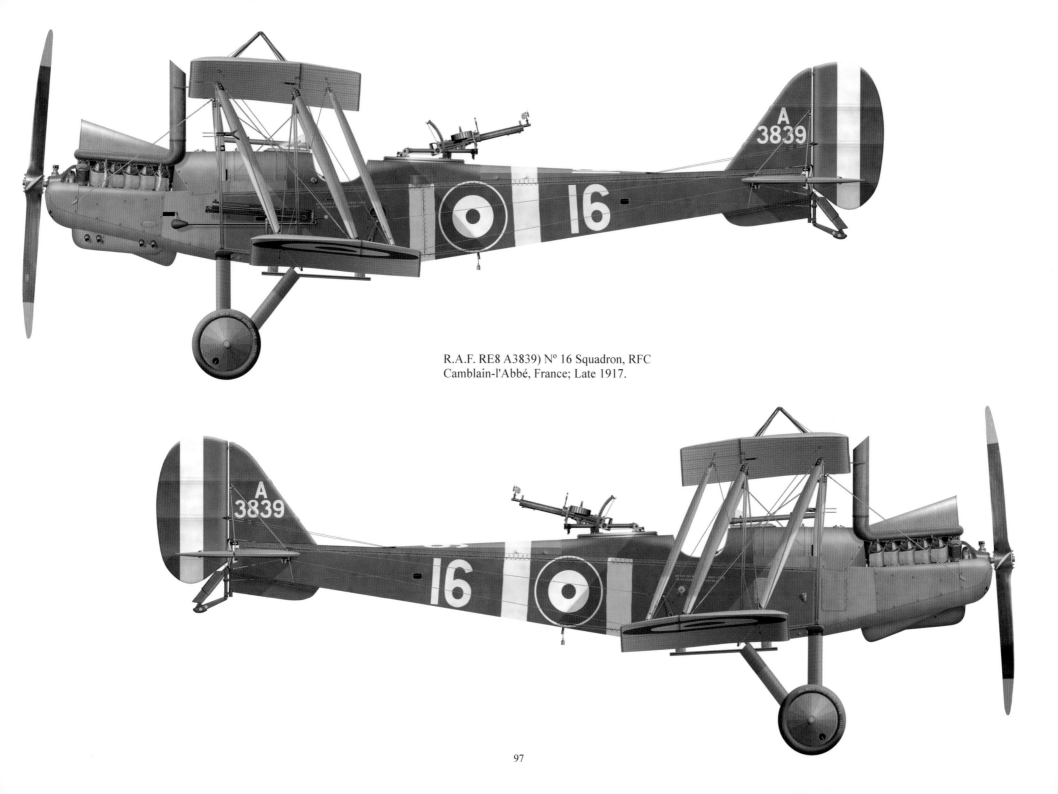

R.A.F. RE8 A3839) Nº 16 Squadron, RFC
Camblain-l'Abbé, France; Late 1917.

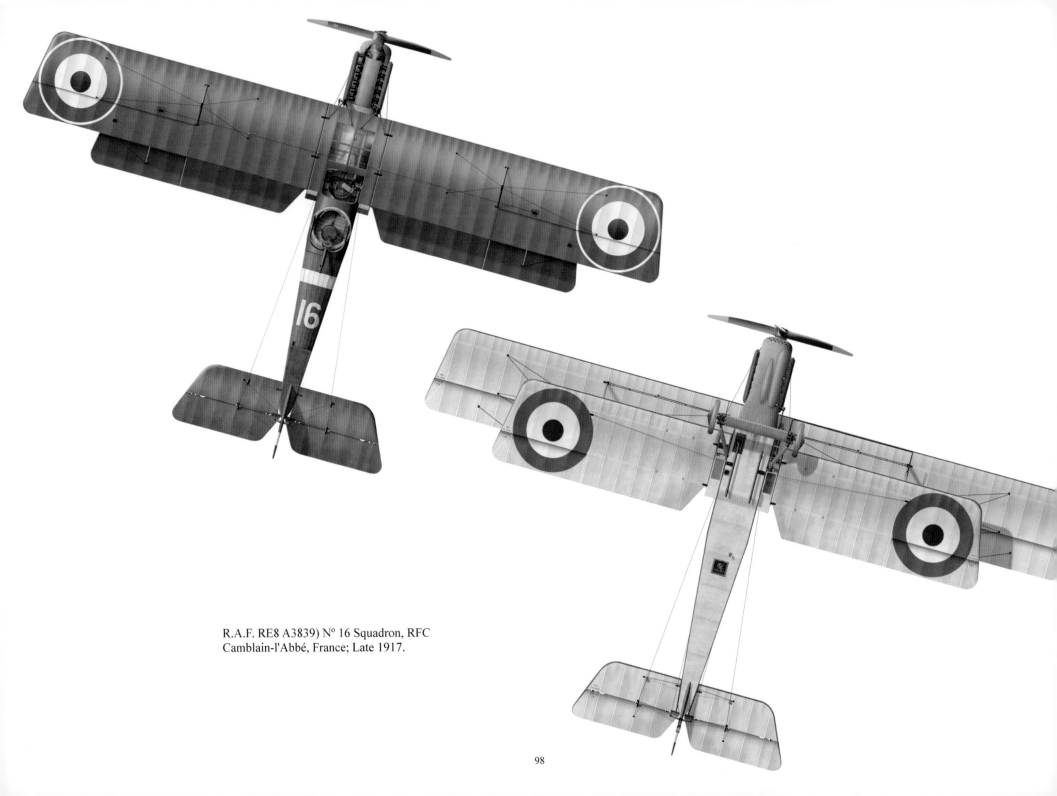

R.A.F. RE8 A3839) Nº 16 Squadron, RFC
Camblain-l'Abbé, France; Late 1917.

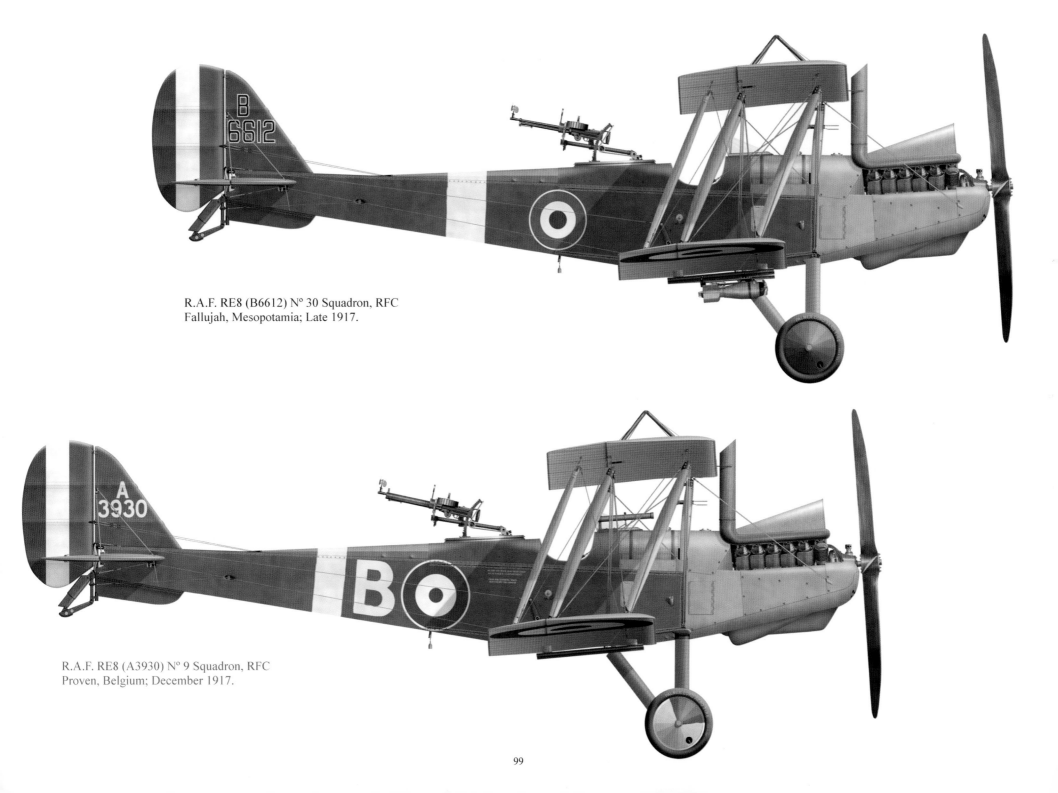

R.A.F. RE8 (B6612) Nº 30 Squadron, RFC
Fallujah, Mesopotamia; Late 1917.

R.A.F. RE8 (A3930) Nº 9 Squadron, RFC
Proven, Belgium; December 1917.

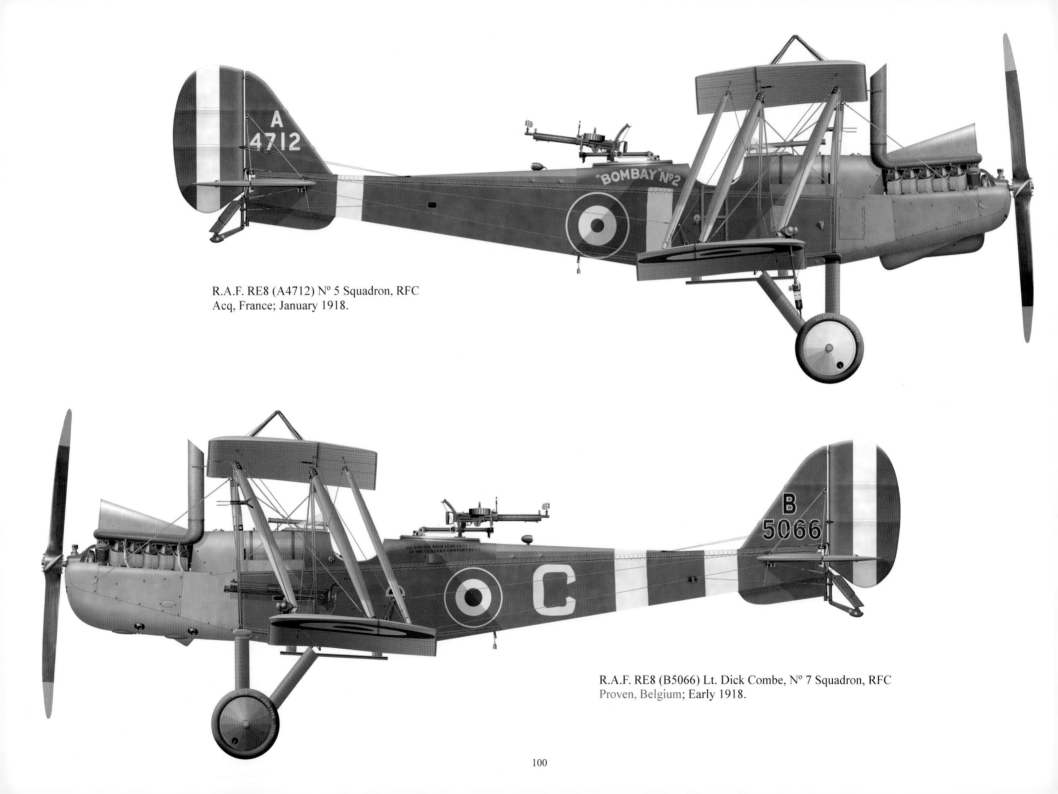

R.A.F. RE8 (A4712) Nº 5 Squadron, RFC
Acq, France; January 1918.

R.A.F. RE8 (B5066) Lt. Dick Combe, Nº 7 Squadron, RFC
Proven, Belgium; Early 1918.

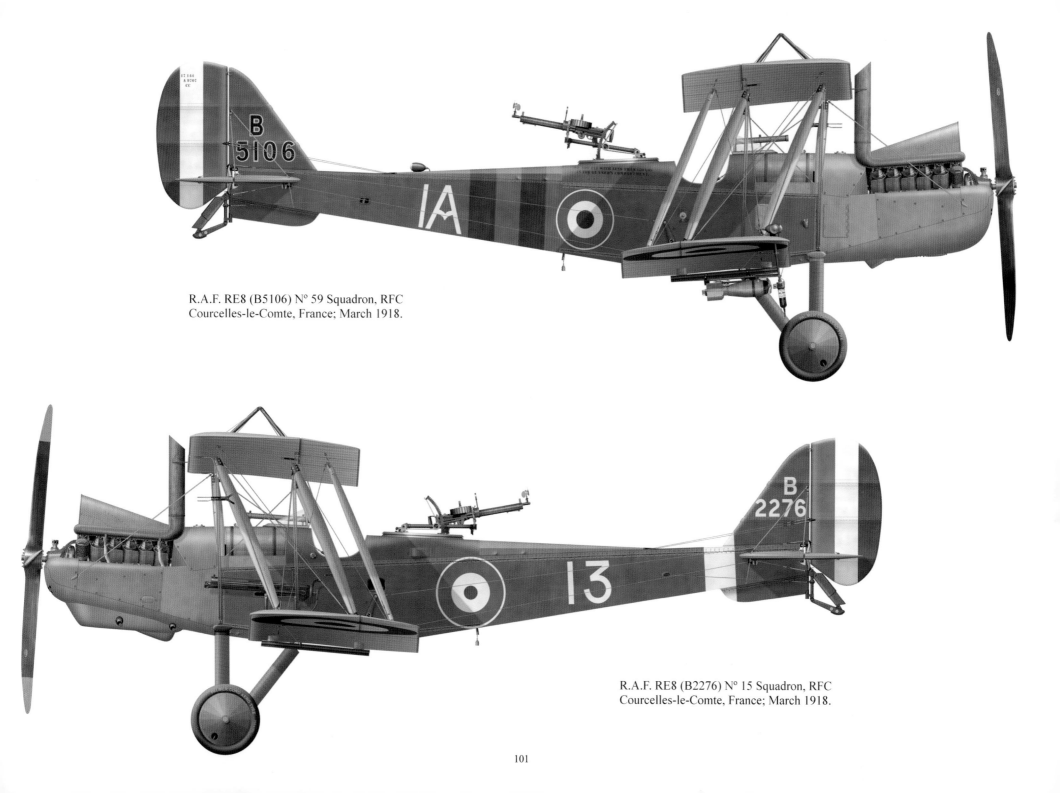

R.A.F. RE8 (B5106) Nº 59 Squadron, RFC
Courcelles-le-Comte, France; March 1918.

R.A.F. RE8 (B2276) Nº 15 Squadron, RFC
Courcelles-le-Comte, France; March 1918.

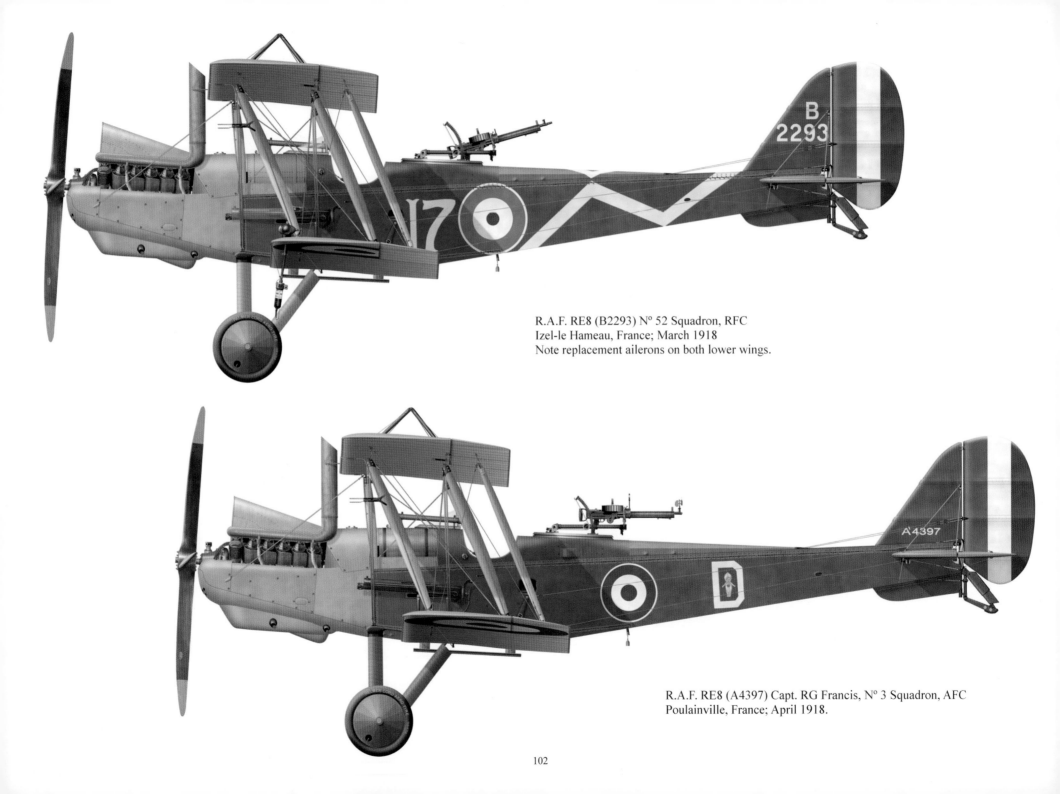

R.A.F. RE8 (B2293) Nº 52 Squadron, RFC
Izel-le Hameau, France; March 1918
Note replacement ailerons on both lower wings.

R.A.F. RE8 (A4397) Capt. RG Francis, Nº 3 Squadron, AFC
Poulainville, France; April 1918.

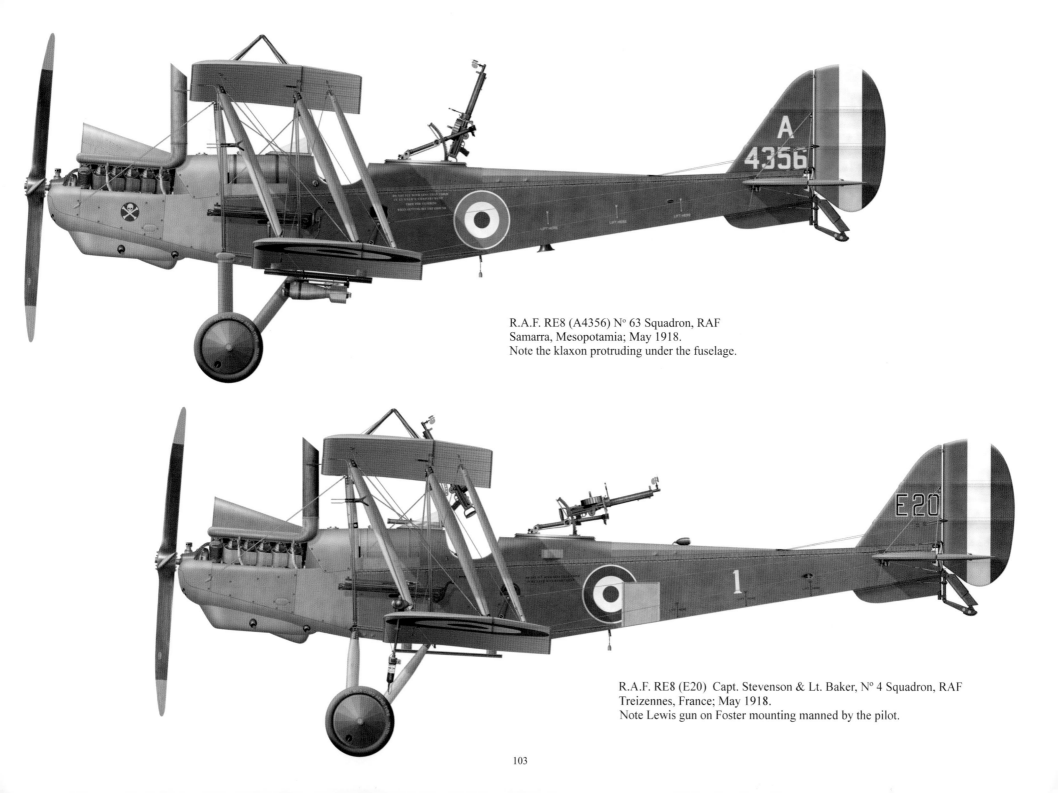

R.A.F. RE8 (A4356) Nº 63 Squadron, RAF
Samarra, Mesopotamia; May 1918.
Note the klaxon protruding under the fuselage.

R.A.F. RE8 (E20) Capt. Stevenson & Lt. Baker, Nº 4 Squadron, RAF
Treizennes, France; May 1918.
Note Lewis gun on Foster mounting manned by the pilot.

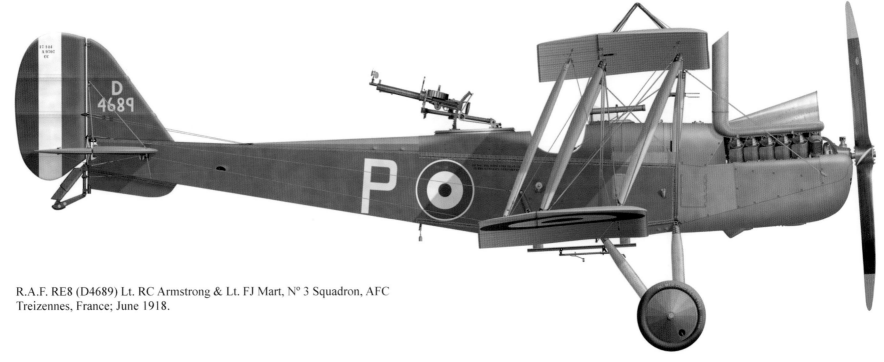

R.A.F. RE8 (D4689) Lt. RC Armstrong & Lt. FJ Mart, Nº 3 Squadron, AFC
Treizennes, France; June 1918.

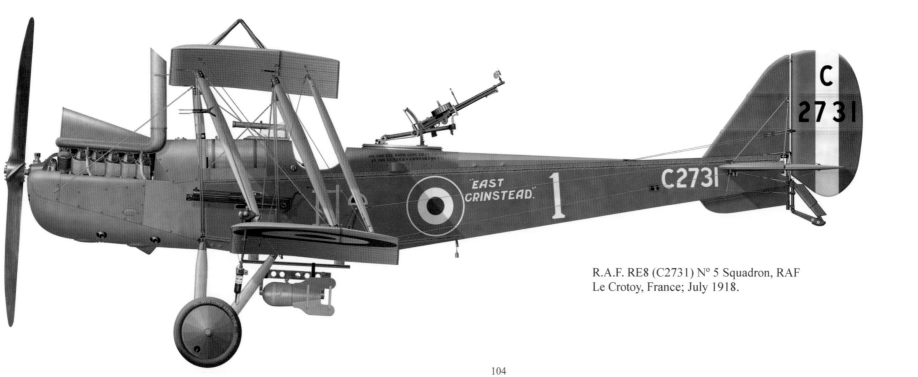

R.A.F. RE8 (C2731) Nº 5 Squadron, RAF
Le Crotoy, France; July 1918.

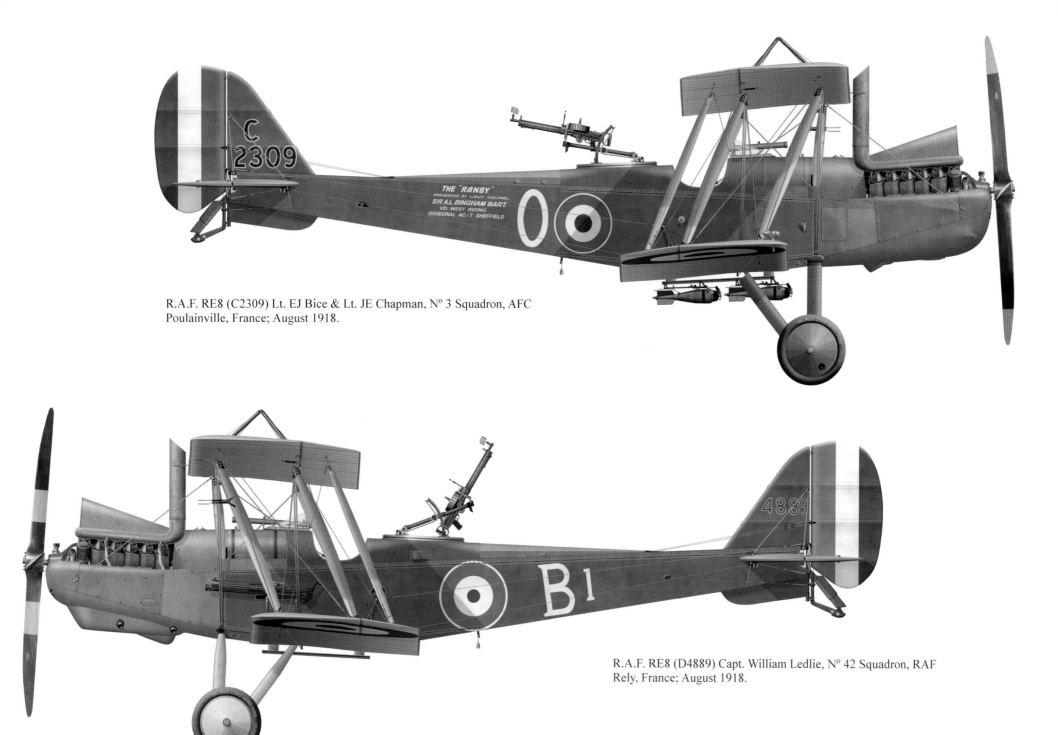

R.A.F. RE8 (C2309) Lt. EJ Bice & Lt. JE Chapman, Nº 3 Squadron, AFC
Poulainville, France; August 1918.

THE "RANBY"
PRESENTED BY LIEUT. COLONEL.
SIR A.L. BINGHAM BART.
VD. WEST RIDING.
DIVISIONAL AC/T SHEFFIELD

R.A.F. RE8 (D4889) Capt. William Ledlie, Nº 42 Squadron, RAF
Rely, France; August 1918.

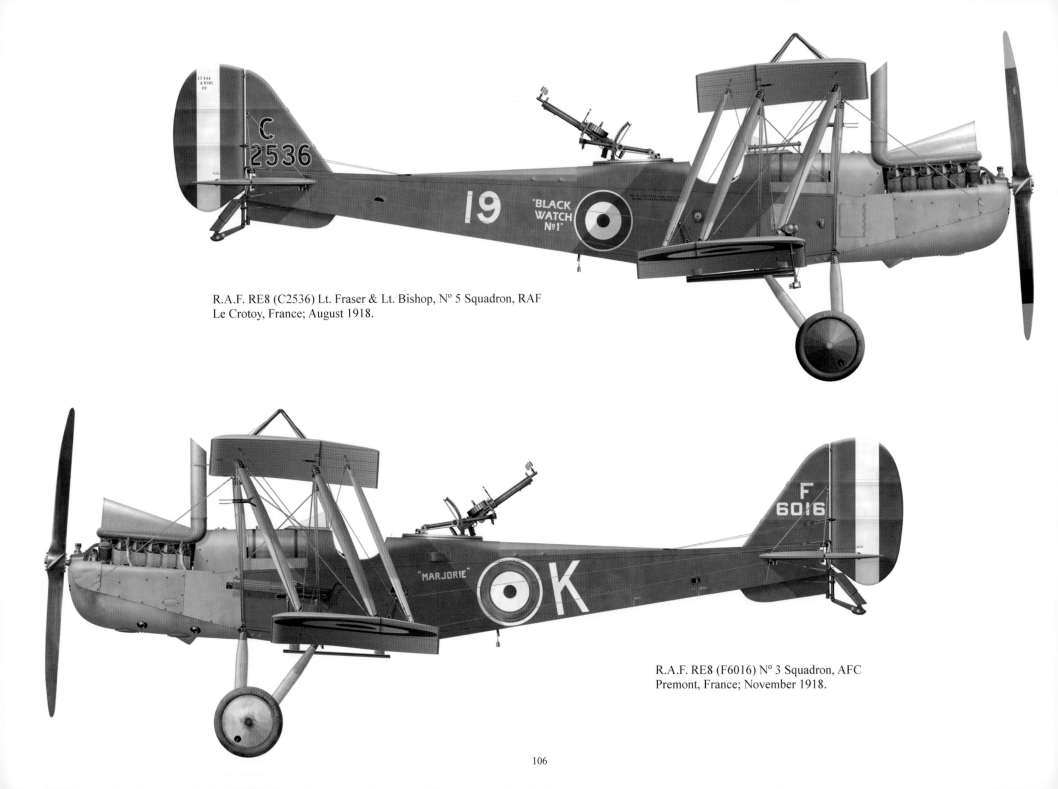

R.A.F. RE8 (C2536) Lt. Fraser & Lt. Bishop, Nº 5 Squadron, RAF
Le Crotoy, France; August 1918.

R.A.F. RE8 (F6016) Nº 3 Squadron, AFC
Premont, France; November 1918.

BRISTOL F2B

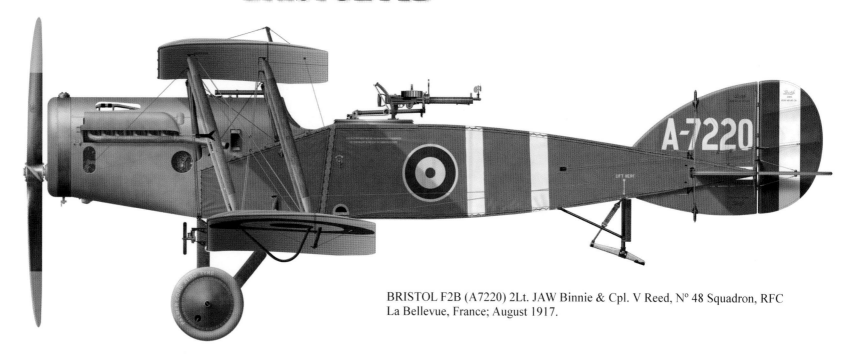

BRISTOL F2B (A7220) 2Lt. JAW Binnie & Cpl. V Reed, N° 48 Squadron, RFC
La Bellevue, France; August 1917.

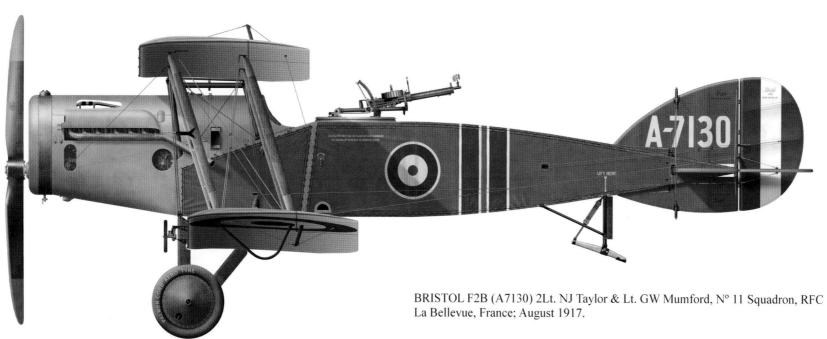

BRISTOL F2B (A7130) 2Lt. NJ Taylor & Lt. GW Mumford, N° 11 Squadron, RFC
La Bellevue, France; August 1917.

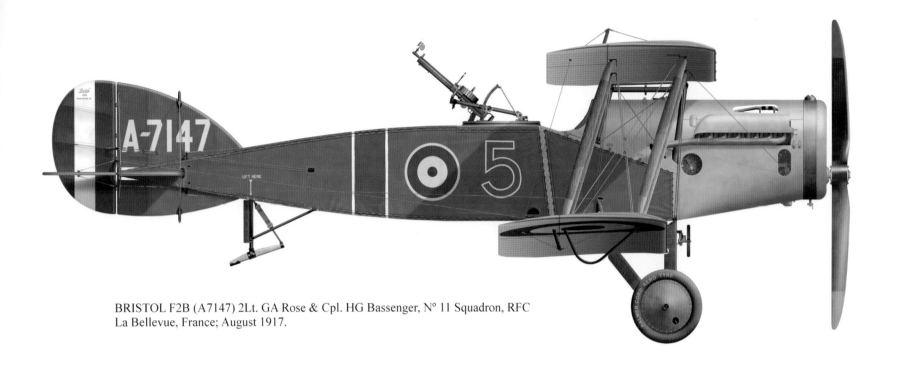

BRISTOL F2B (A7147) 2Lt. GA Rose & Cpl. HG Bassenger, N° 11 Squadron, RFC
La Bellevue, France; August 1917.

BRISTOL F2B (A7131) N° 11 Squadron, RFC
La Bellevue, France; September 1917.

BRISTOL F2B (A7127) 2Lt. AE Turvey & 2Lt. AMW Hewitt, Nº 11 Squadron, RFC
La Bellevue, France; October 1917.

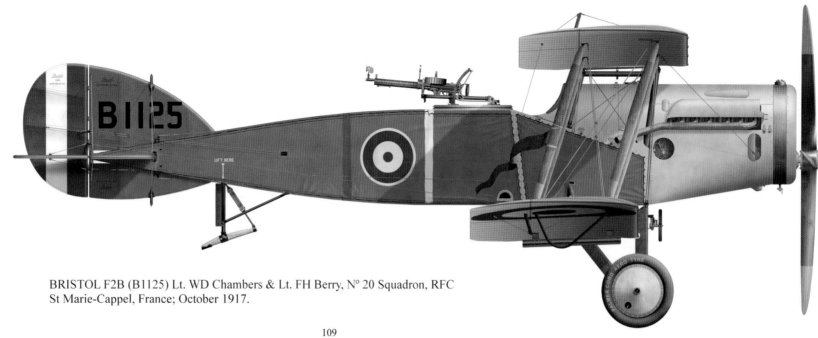

BRISTOL F2B (B1125) Lt. WD Chambers & Lt. FH Berry, Nº 20 Squadron, RFC
St Marie-Cappel, France; October 1917.

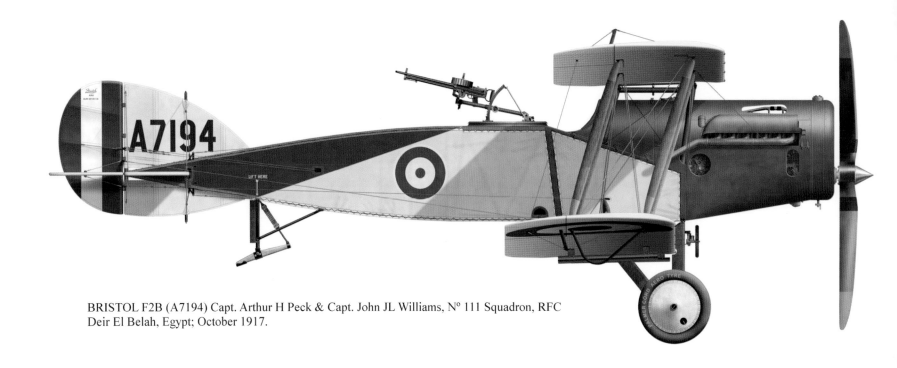

BRISTOL F2B (A7194) Capt. Arthur H Peck & Capt. John JL Williams, Nº 111 Squadron, RFC
Deir El Belah, Egypt; October 1917.

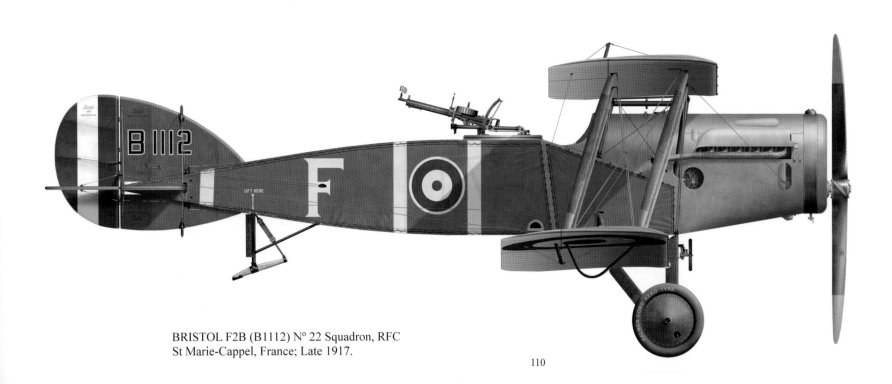

BRISTOL F2B (B1112) Nº 22 Squadron, RFC
St Marie-Cappel, France; Late 1917.

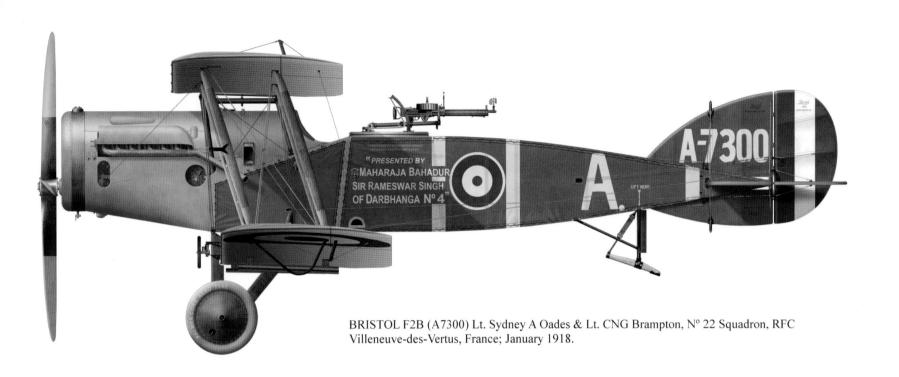

BRISTOL F2B (A7300) Lt. Sydney A Oades & Lt. CNG Brampton, Nº 22 Squadron, RFC
Villeneuve-des-Vertus, France; January 1918.

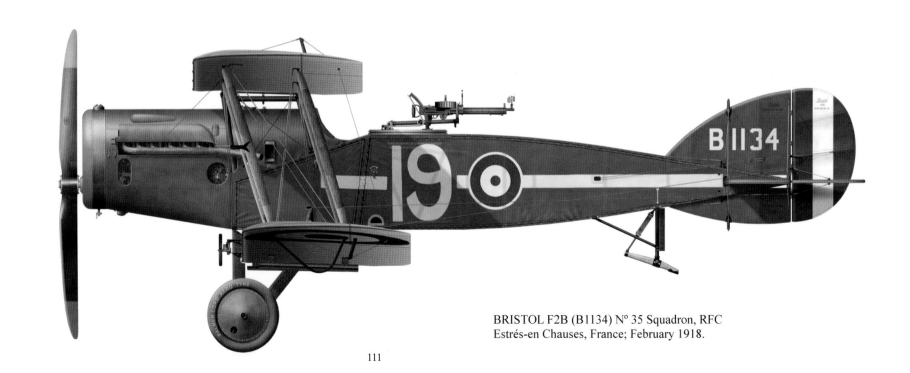

BRISTOL F2B (B1134) Nº 35 Squadron, RFC
Estrés-en Chauses, France; February 1918.

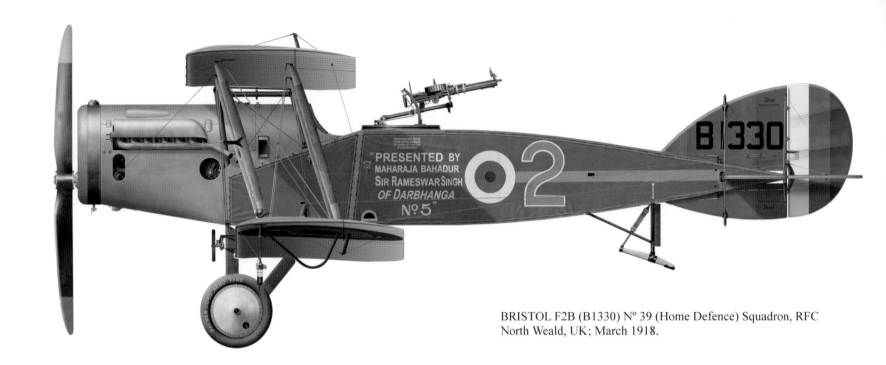

BRISTOL F2B (B1330) Nº 39 (Home Defence) Squadron, RFC
North Weald, UK; March 1918.

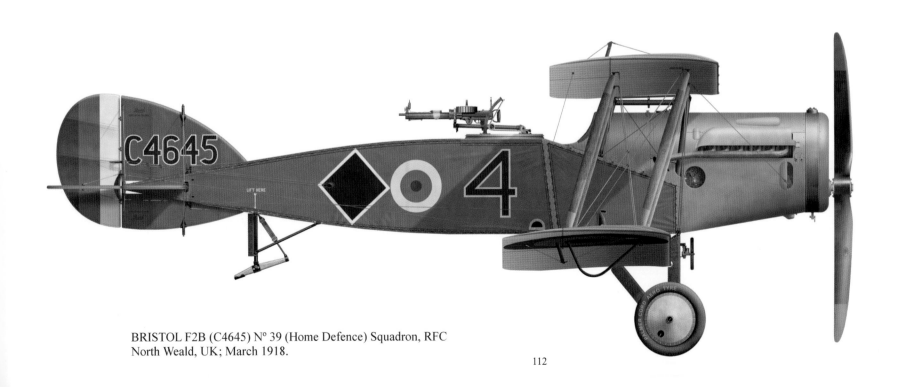

BRISTOL F2B (C4645) Nº 39 (Home Defence) Squadron, RFC
North Weald, UK; March 1918.

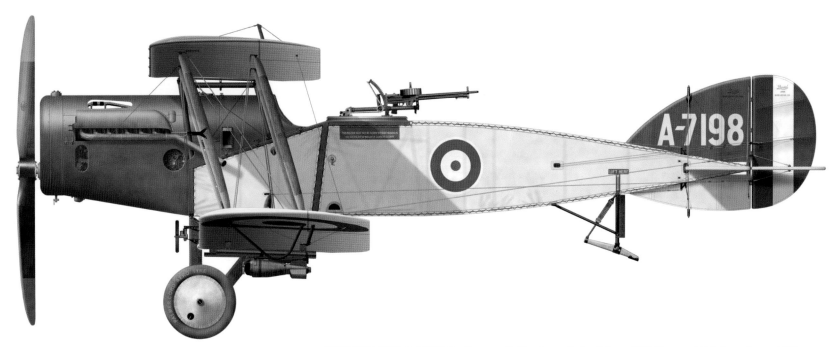

BRISTOL F2B (A7198) Lt. Eustace S Headman & Lt. Edward BS Braton, N° 1 Squadron, AFC
El Mejdel, Egypt, March 1918.

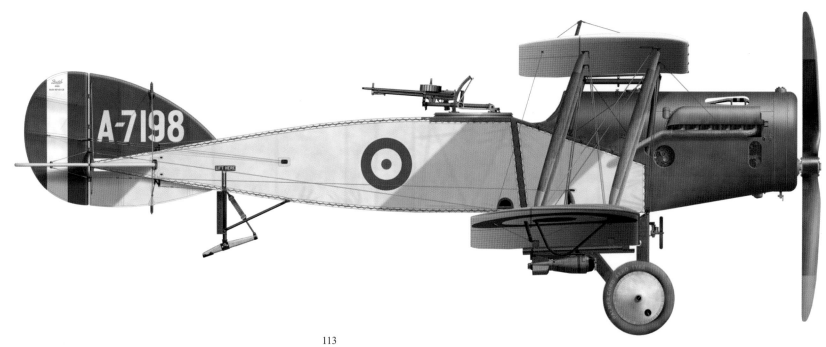

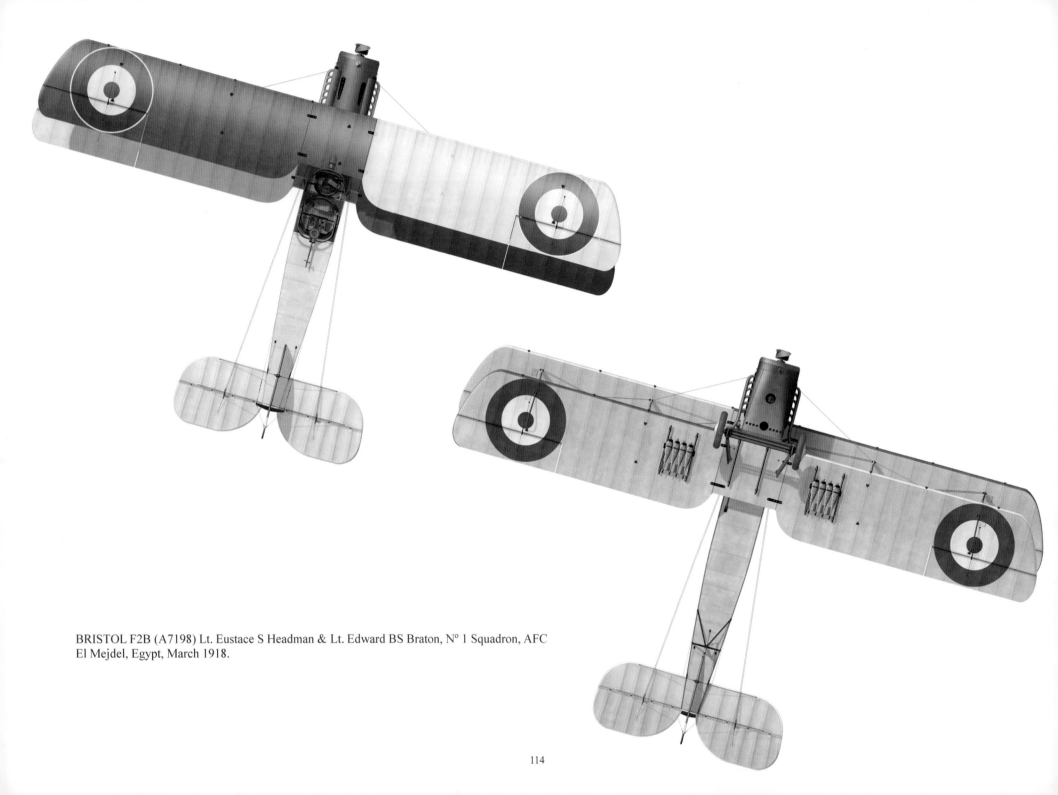

BRISTOL F2B (A7198) Lt. Eustace S Headman & Lt. Edward BS Braton, N° 1 Squadron, AFC
El Mejdel, Egypt, March 1918.

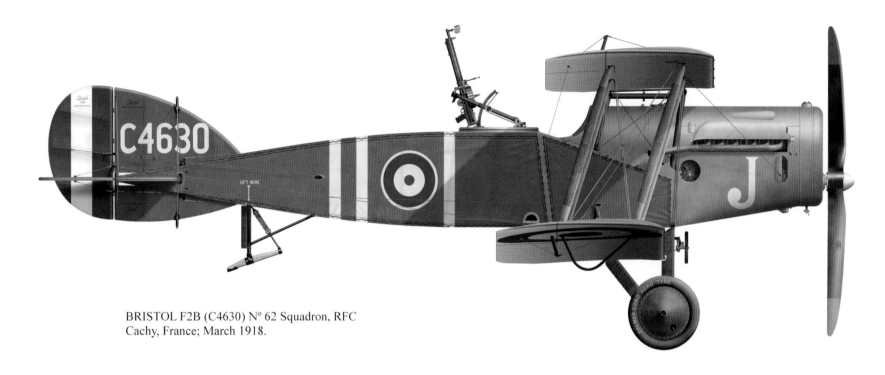

BRISTOL F2B (C4630) N° 62 Squadron, RFC
Cachy, France; March 1918.

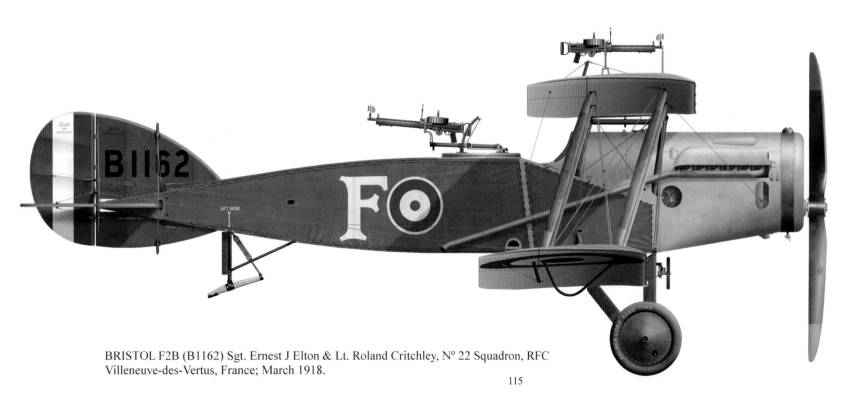

BRISTOL F2B (B1162) Sgt. Ernest J Elton & Lt. Roland Critchley, N° 22 Squadron, RFC
Villeneuve-des-Vertus, France; March 1918.

115

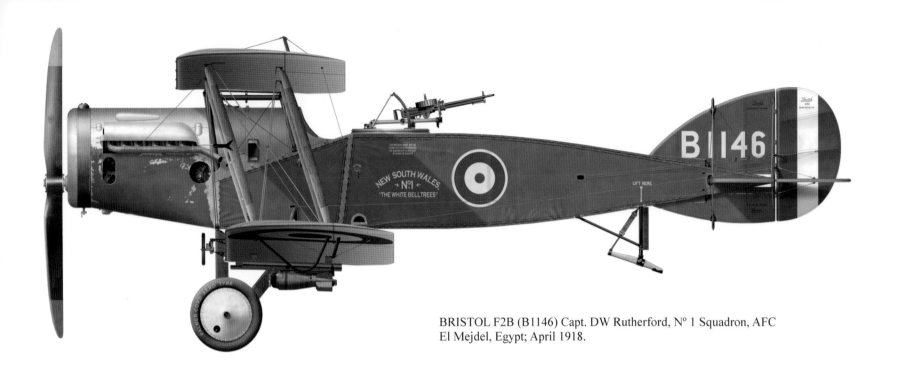

BRISTOL F2B (B1146) Capt. DW Rutherford, N° 1 Squadron, AFC
El Mejdel, Egypt; April 1918.

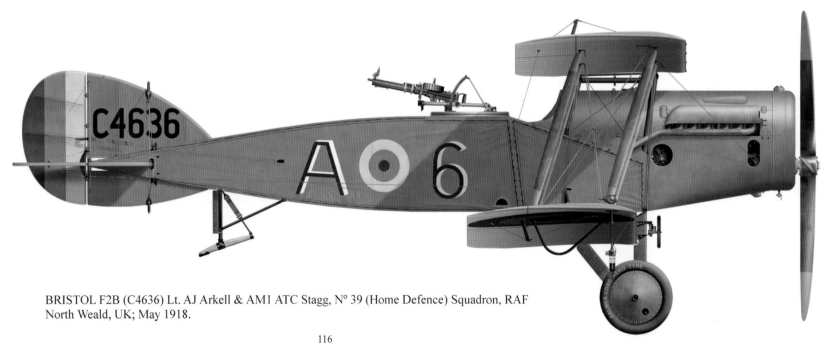

BRISTOL F2B (C4636) Lt. AJ Arkell & AM1 ATC Stagg, N° 39 (Home Defence) Squadron, RAF
North Weald, UK; May 1918.

BRISTOL F2B (D7939) Lt. Victor E Groom & 2Lt. Ernest Hardcastle, Nº 20 Squadron, RAF
Boisdinghem, France; July 1918.

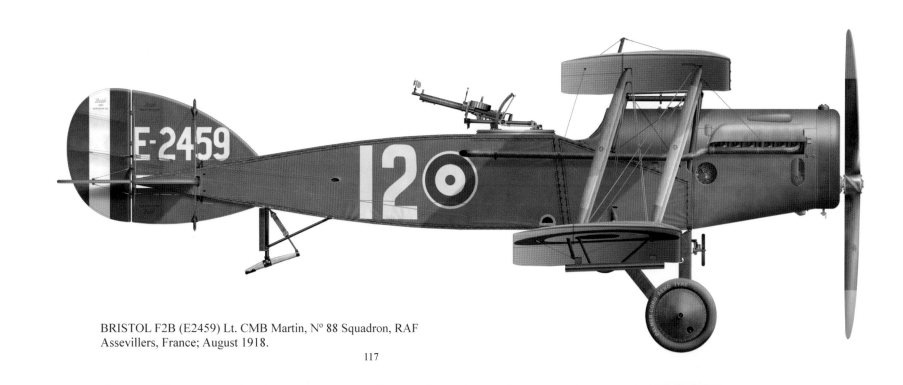

BRISTOL F2B (E2459) Lt. CMB Martin, Nº 88 Squadron, RAF
Assevillers, France; August 1918.

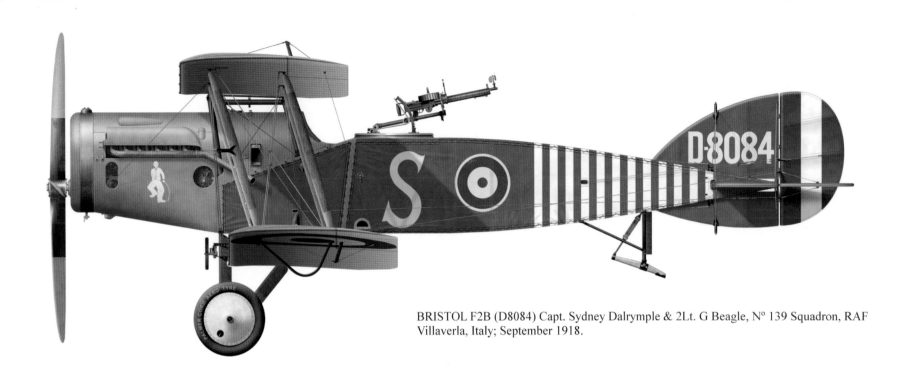

BRISTOL F2B (D8084) Capt. Sydney Dalrymple & 2Lt. G Beagle, Nº 139 Squadron, RAF
Villaverla, Italy; September 1918.

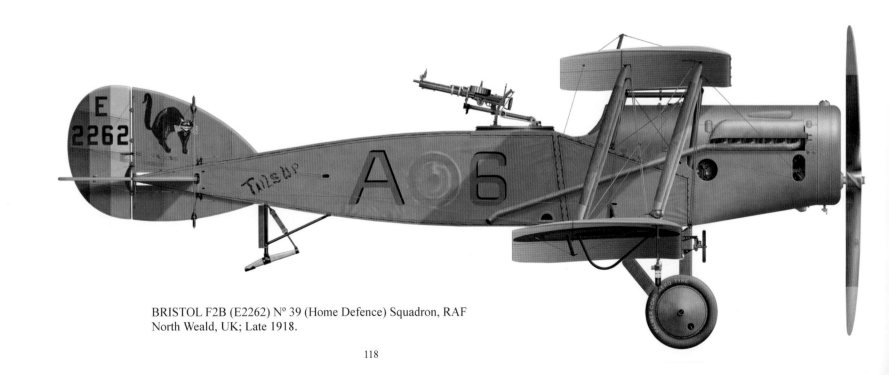

BRISTOL F2B (E2262) Nº 39 (Home Defence) Squadron, RAF
North Weald, UK; Late 1918.

A.M.C. DH9

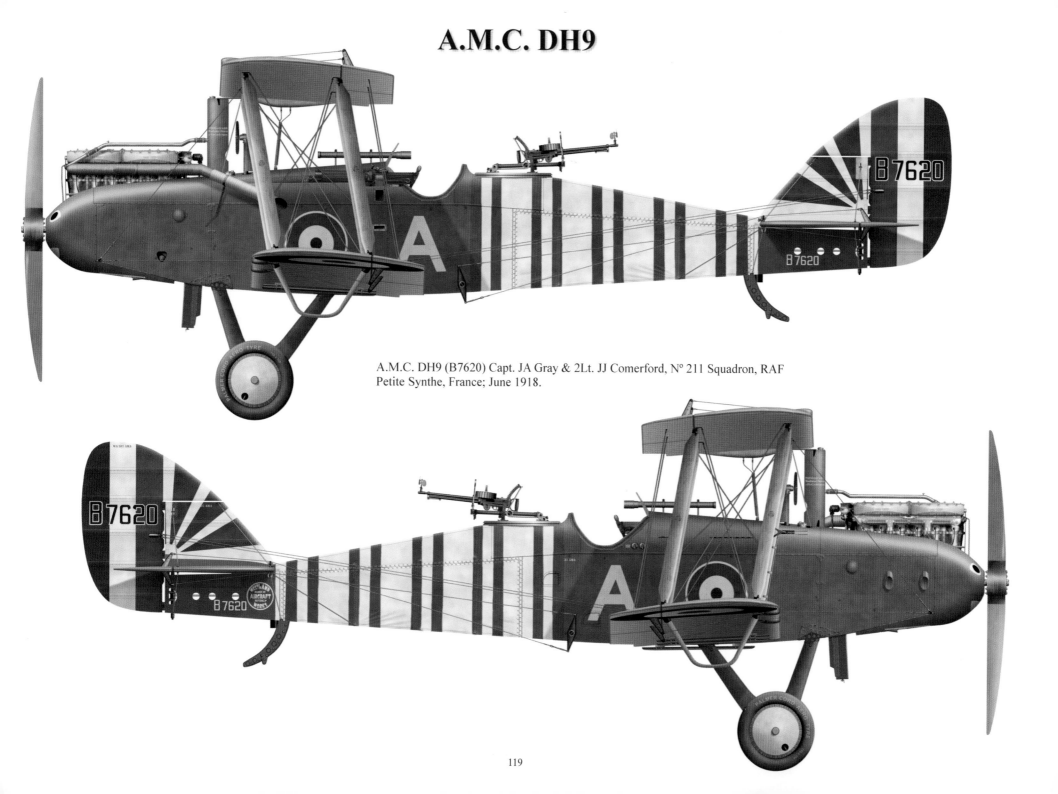

A.M.C. DH9 (B7620) Capt. JA Gray & 2Lt. JJ Comerford, N° 211 Squadron, RAF
Petite Synthe, France; June 1918.

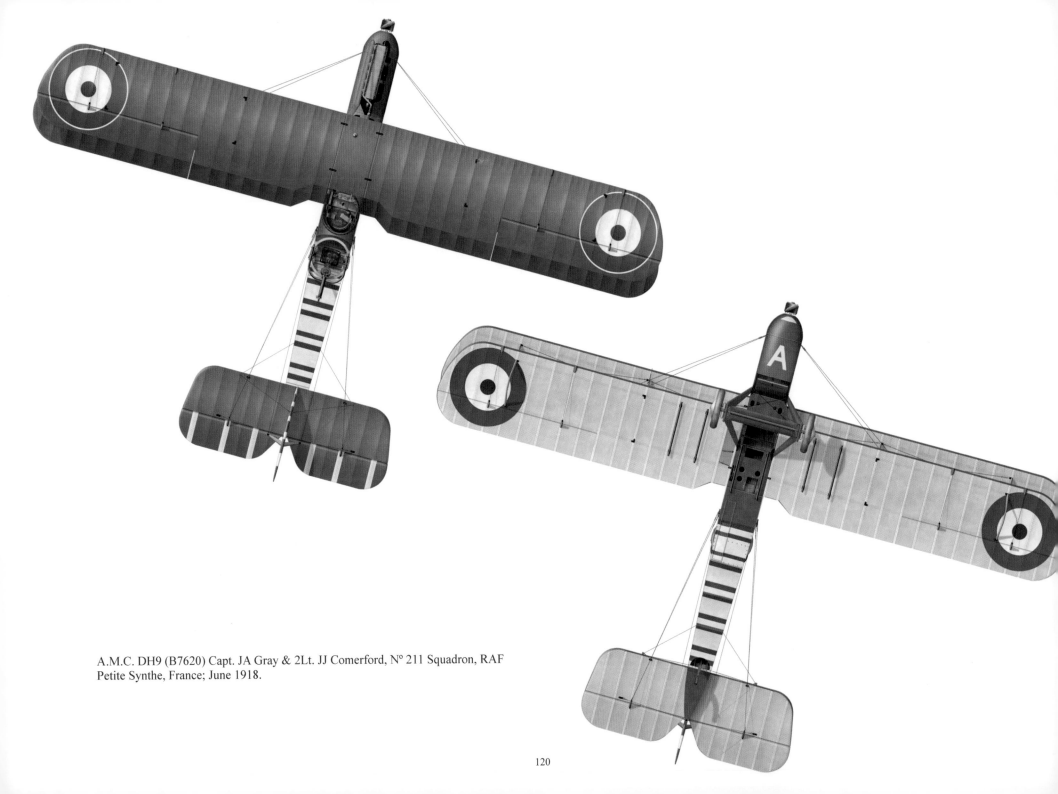

A.M.C. DH9 (B7620) Capt. JA Gray & 2Lt. JJ Comerford, Nº 211 Squadron, RAF
Petite Synthe, France; June 1918.

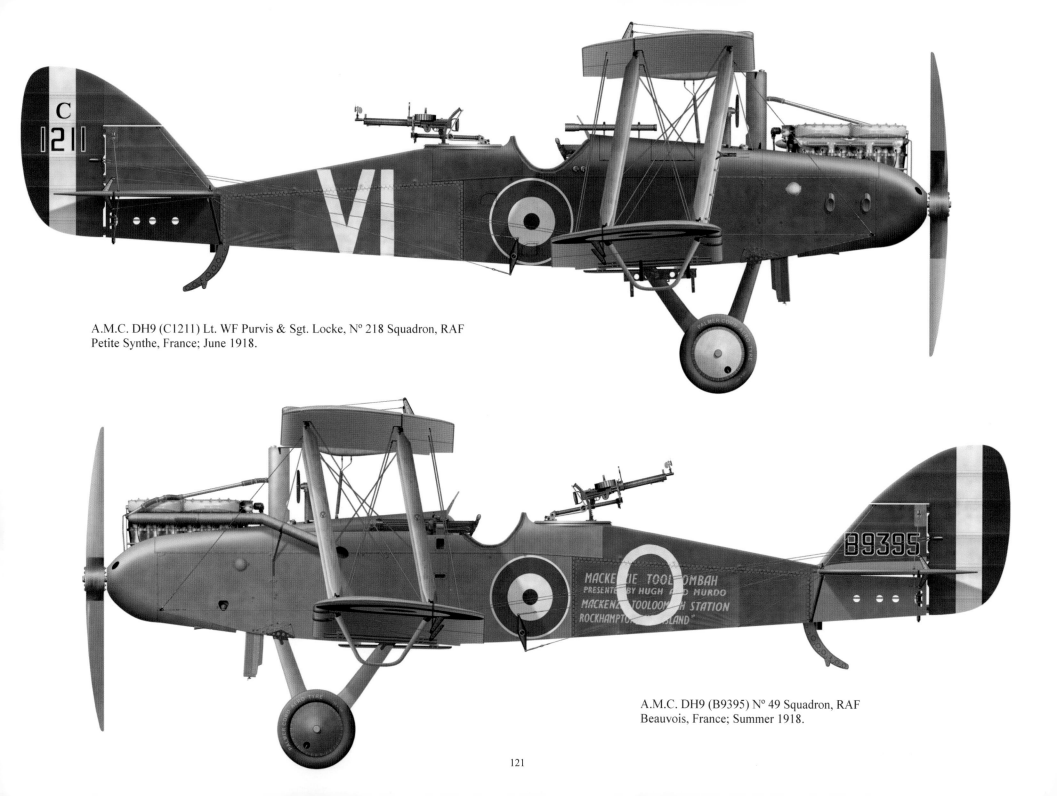

A.M.C. DH9 (C1211) Lt. WF Purvis & Sgt. Locke, Nº 218 Squadron, RAF
Petite Synthe, France; June 1918.

A.M.C. DH9 (B9395) Nº 49 Squadron, RAF
Beauvois, France; Summer 1918.

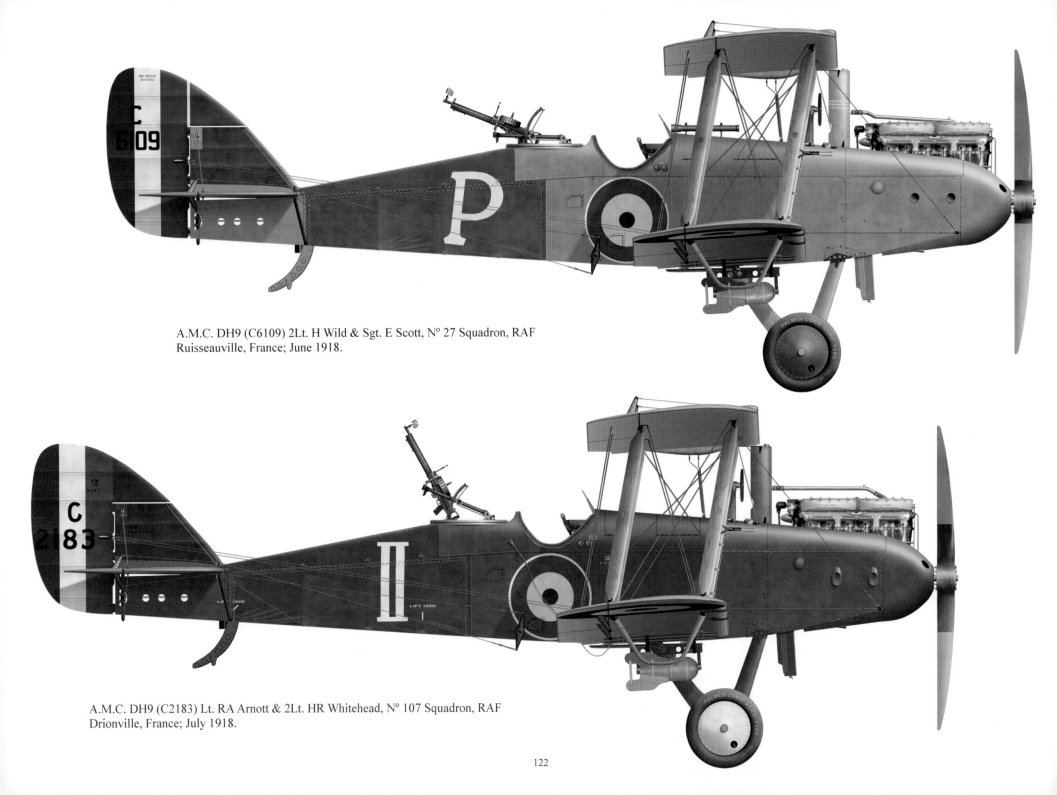

A.M.C. DH9 (C6109) 2Lt. H Wild & Sgt. E Scott, Nº 27 Squadron, RAF
Ruisseauville, France; June 1918.

A.M.C. DH9 (C2183) Lt. RA Arnott & 2Lt. HR Whitehead, Nº 107 Squadron, RAF
Drionville, France; July 1918.

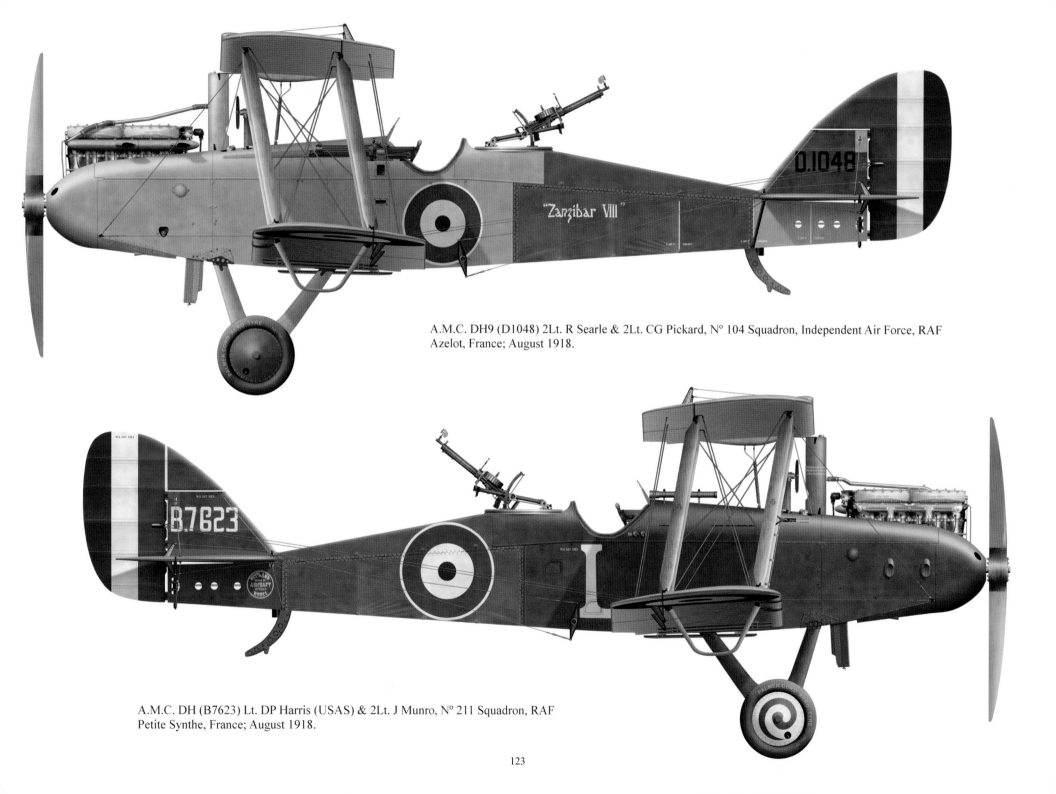

A.M.C. DH9 (D1048) 2Lt. R Searle & 2Lt. CG Pickard, N° 104 Squadron, Independent Air Force, RAF
Azelot, France; August 1918.

A.M.C. DH (B7623) Lt. DP Harris (USAS) & 2Lt. J Munro, N° 211 Squadron, RAF
Petite Synthe, France; August 1918.

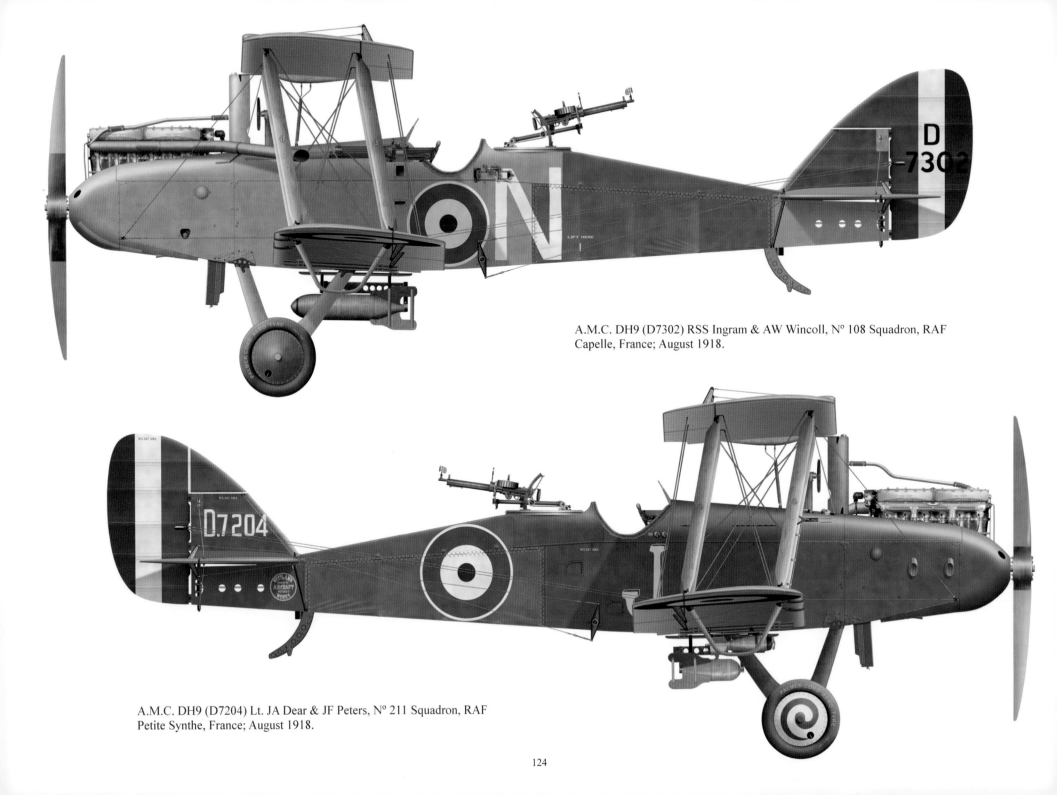

A.M.C. DH9 (D7302) RSS Ingram & AW Wincoll, Nº 108 Squadron, RAF
Capelle, France; August 1918.

A.M.C. DH9 (D7204) Lt. JA Dear & JF Peters, Nº 211 Squadron, RAF
Petite Synthe, France; August 1918.

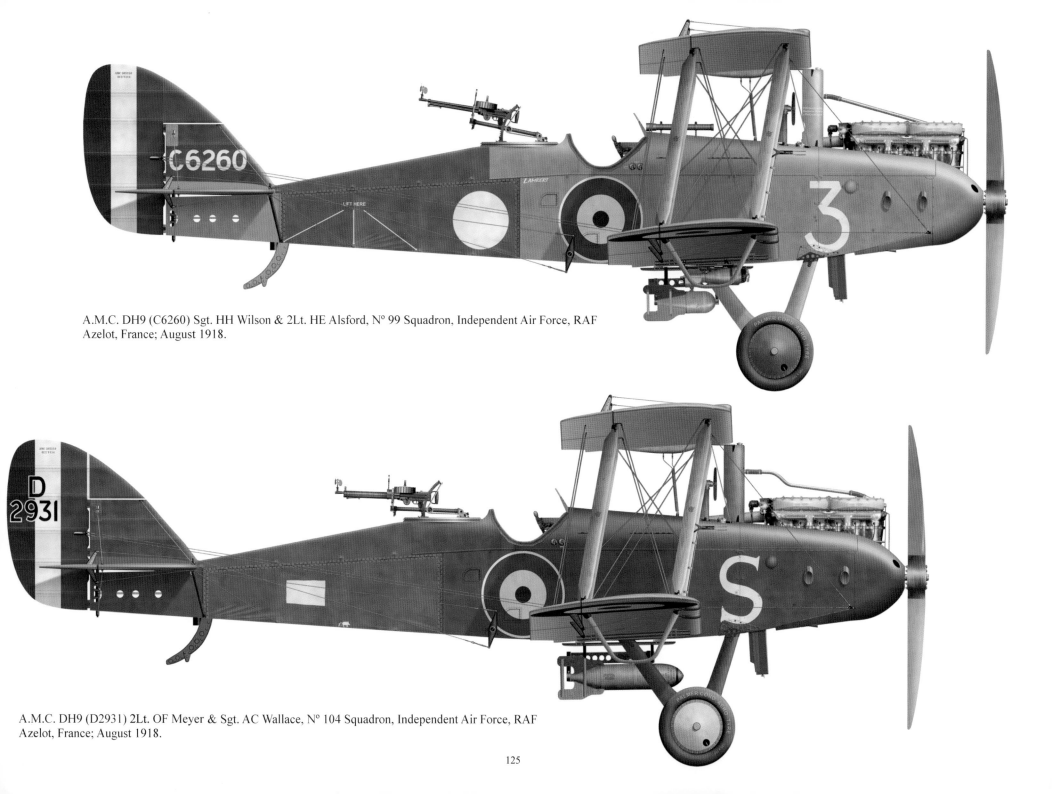

A.M.C. DH9 (C6260) Sgt. HH Wilson & 2Lt. HE Alsford, Nº 99 Squadron, Independent Air Force, RAF
Azelot, France; August 1918.

A.M.C. DH9 (D2931) 2Lt. OF Meyer & Sgt. AC Wallace, Nº 104 Squadron, Independent Air Force, RAF
Azelot, France; August 1918.

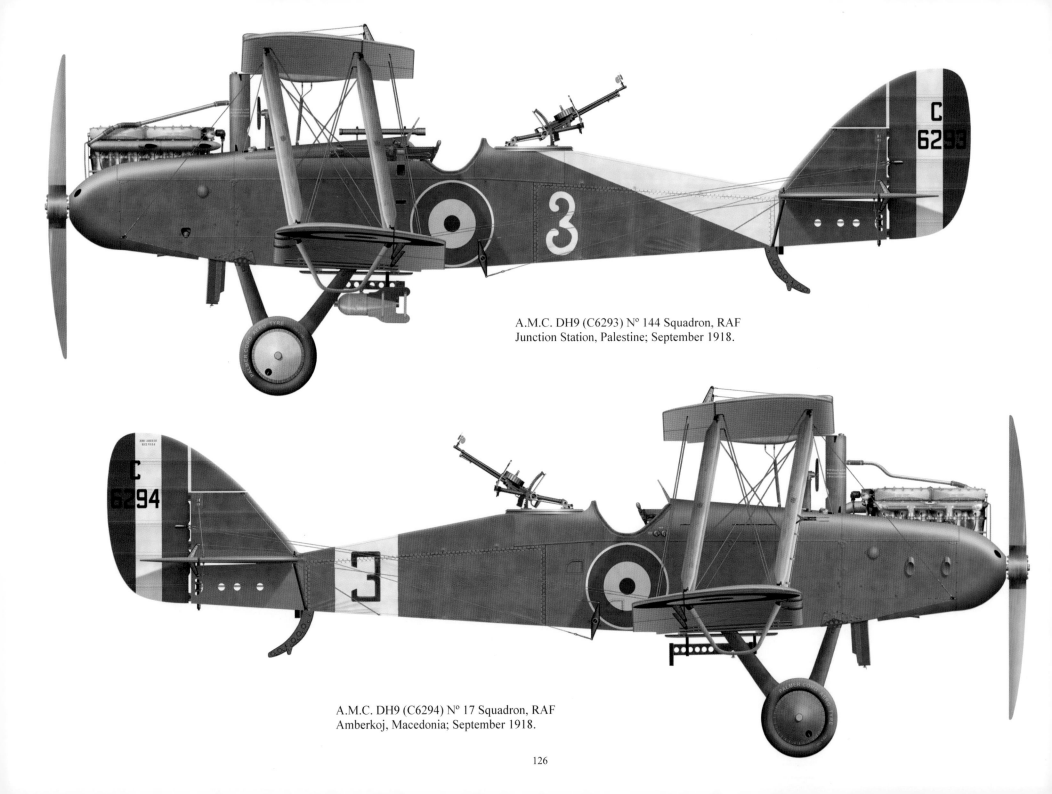

A.M.C. DH9 (C6293) Nº 144 Squadron, RAF
Junction Station, Palestine; September 1918.

A.M.C. DH9 (C6294) Nº 17 Squadron, RAF
Amberkoj, Macedonia; September 1918.

126

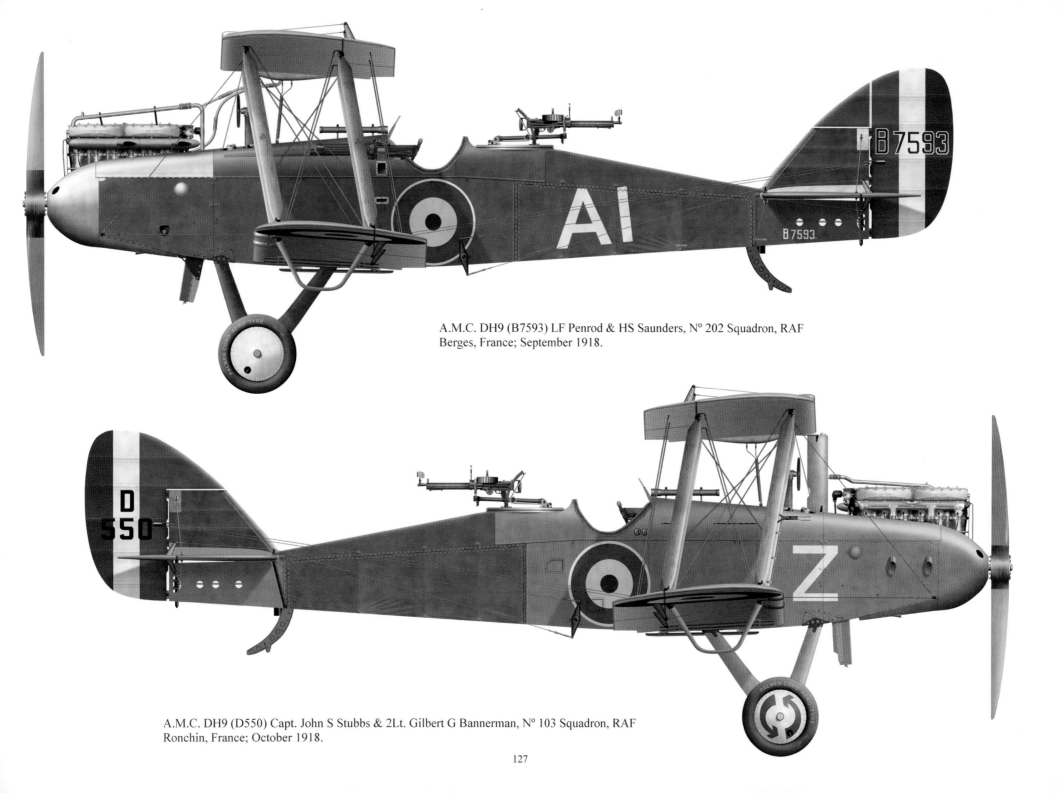

A.M.C. DH9 (B7593) LF Penrod & HS Saunders, Nº 202 Squadron, RAF
Berges, France; September 1918.

A.M.C. DH9 (D550) Capt. John S Stubbs & 2Lt. Gilbert G Bannerman, Nº 103 Squadron, RAF
Ronchin, France; October 1918.

A.M.C. DH9A

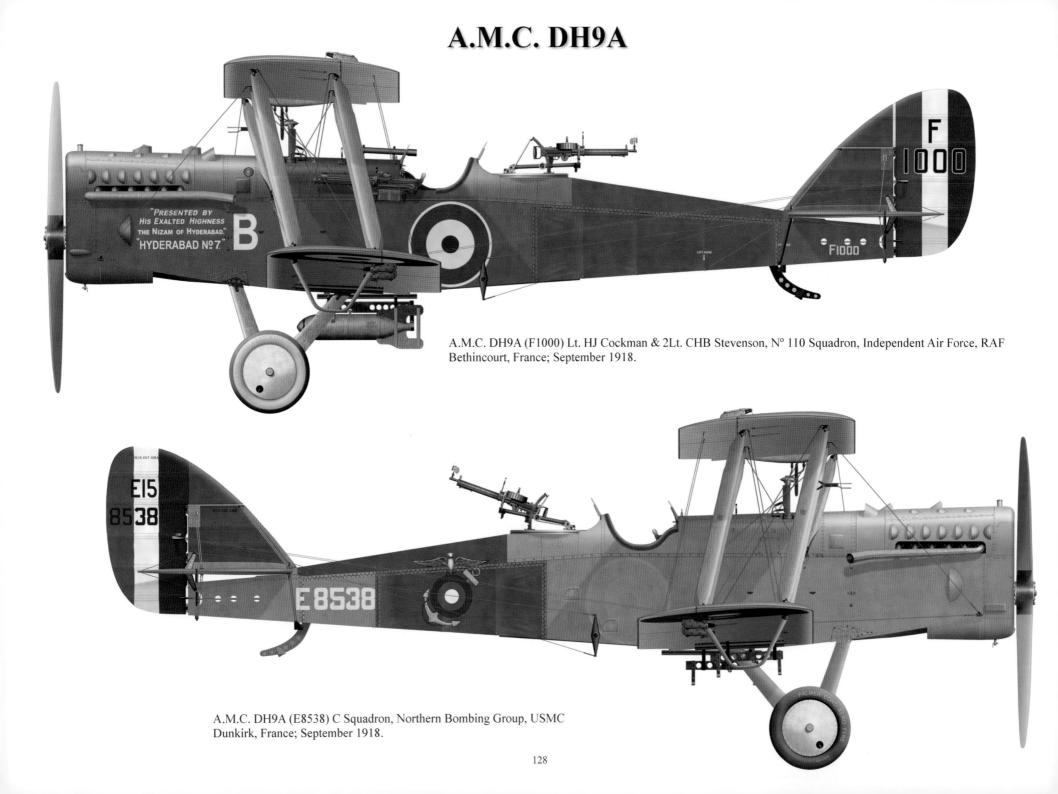

A.M.C. DH9A (F1000) Lt. HJ Cockman & 2Lt. CHB Stevenson, Nº 110 Squadron, Independent Air Force, RAF Bethincourt, France; September 1918.

A.M.C. DH9A (E8538) C Squadron, Northern Bombing Group, USMC Dunkirk, France; September 1918.

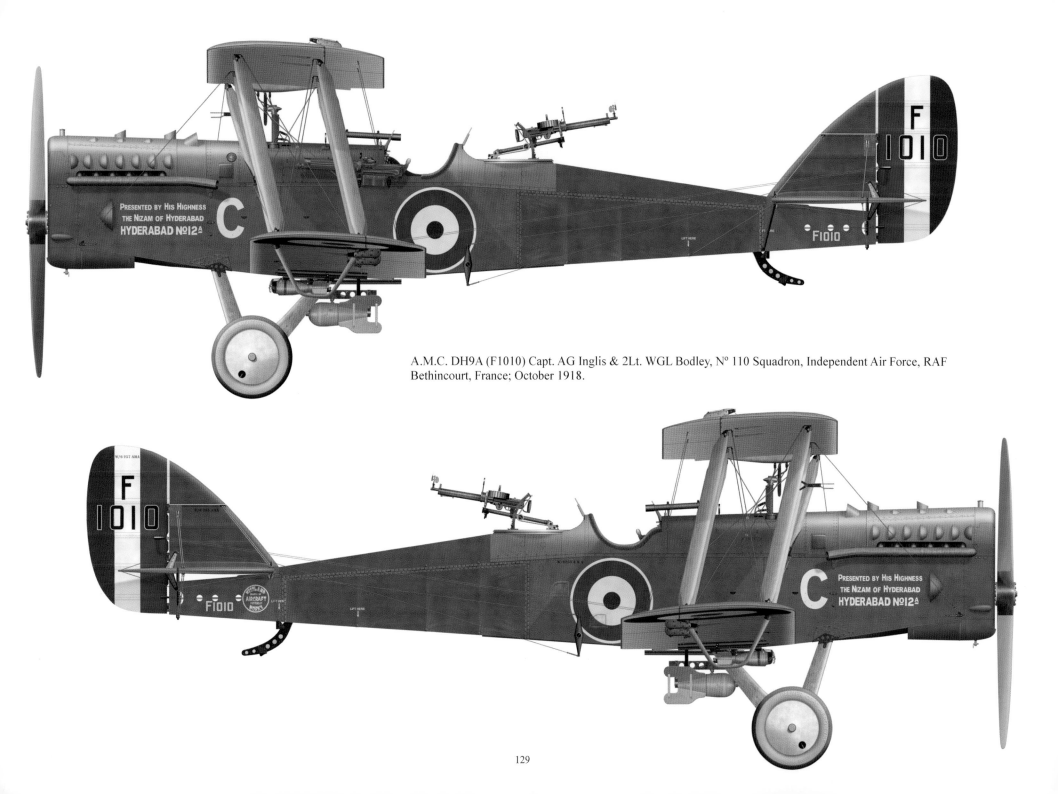

A.M.C. DH9A (F1010) Capt. AG Inglis & 2Lt. WGL Bodley, Nº 110 Squadron, Independent Air Force, RAF Bethincourt, France; October 1918.

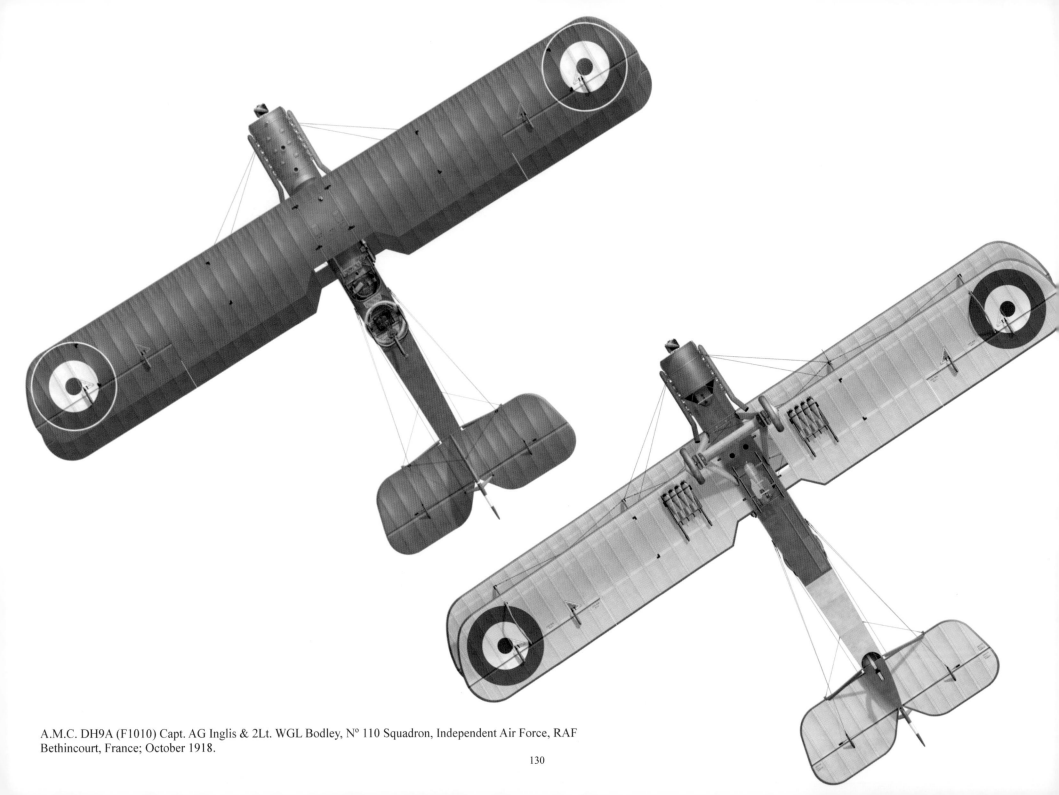

A.M.C. DH9A (F1010) Capt. AG Inglis & 2Lt. WGL Bodley, Nº 110 Squadron, Independent Air Force, RAF
Bethincourt, France; October 1918.

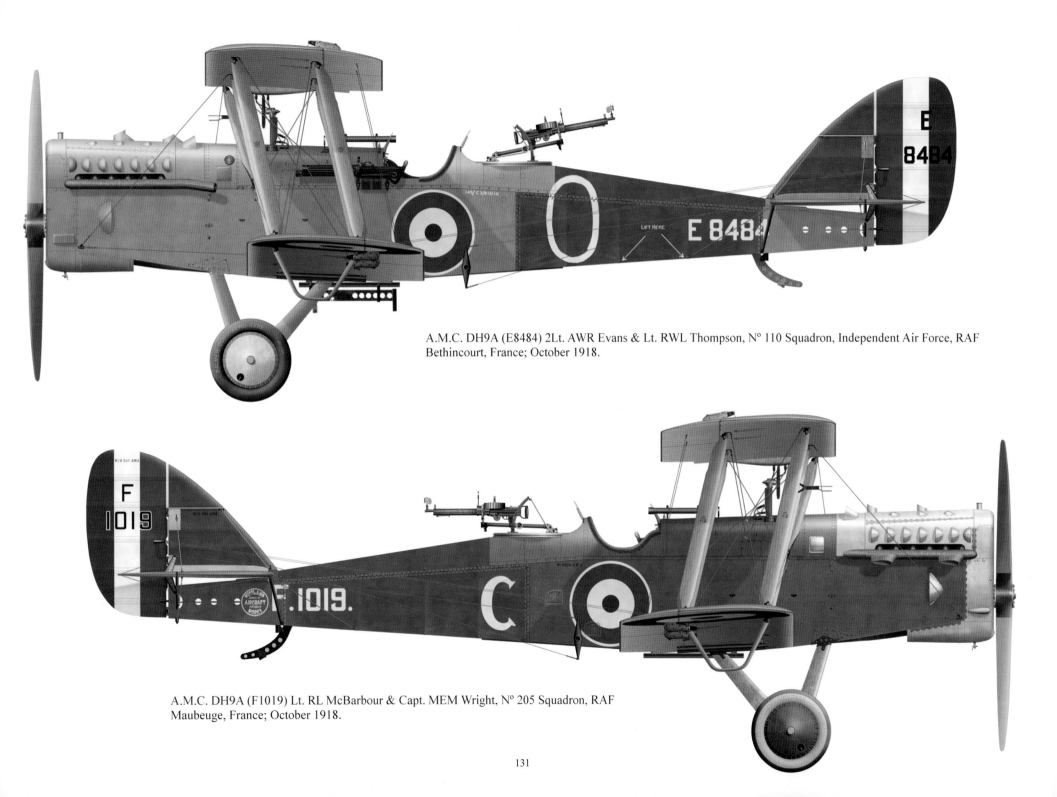

A.M.C. DH9A (E8484) 2Lt. AWR Evans & Lt. RWL Thompson, N° 110 Squadron, Independent Air Force, RAF
Bethincourt, France; October 1918.

A.M.C. DH9A (F1019) Lt. RL McBarbour & Capt. MEM Wright, N° 205 Squadron, RAF
Maubeuge, France; October 1918.

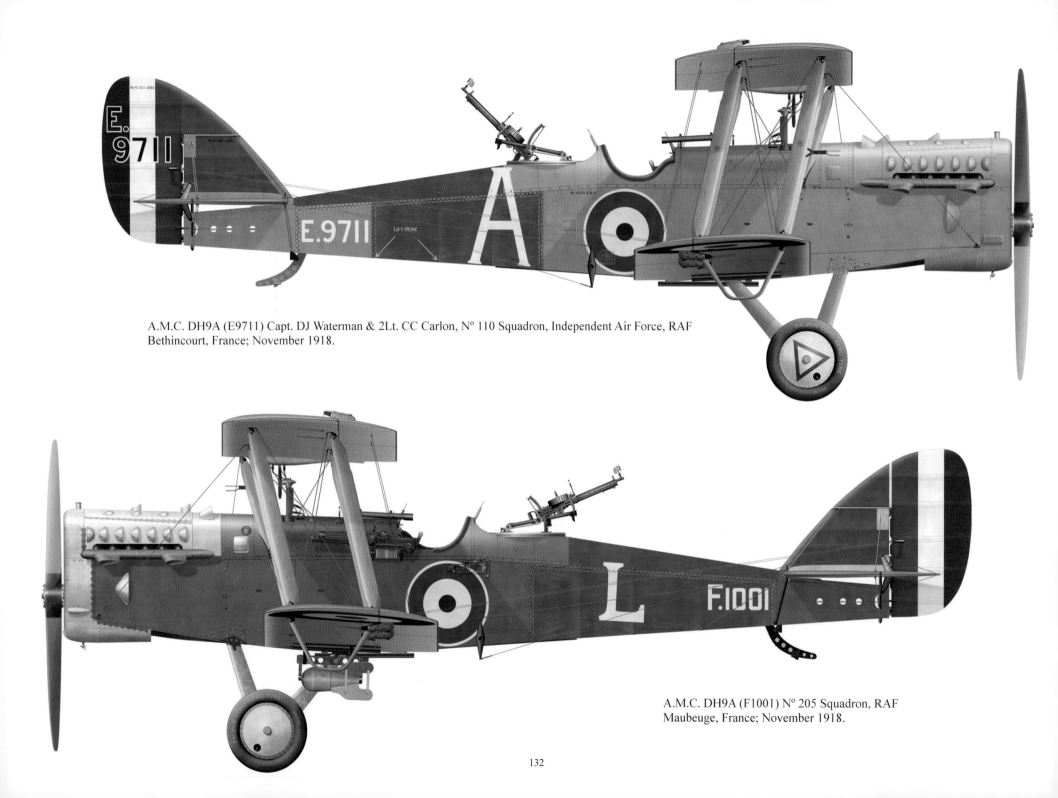

A.M.C. DH9A (E9711) Capt. DJ Waterman & 2Lt. CC Carlon, Nº 110 Squadron, Independent Air Force, RAF Bethincourt, France; November 1918.

A.M.C. DH9A (F1001) Nº 205 Squadron, RAF Maubeuge, France; November 1918.

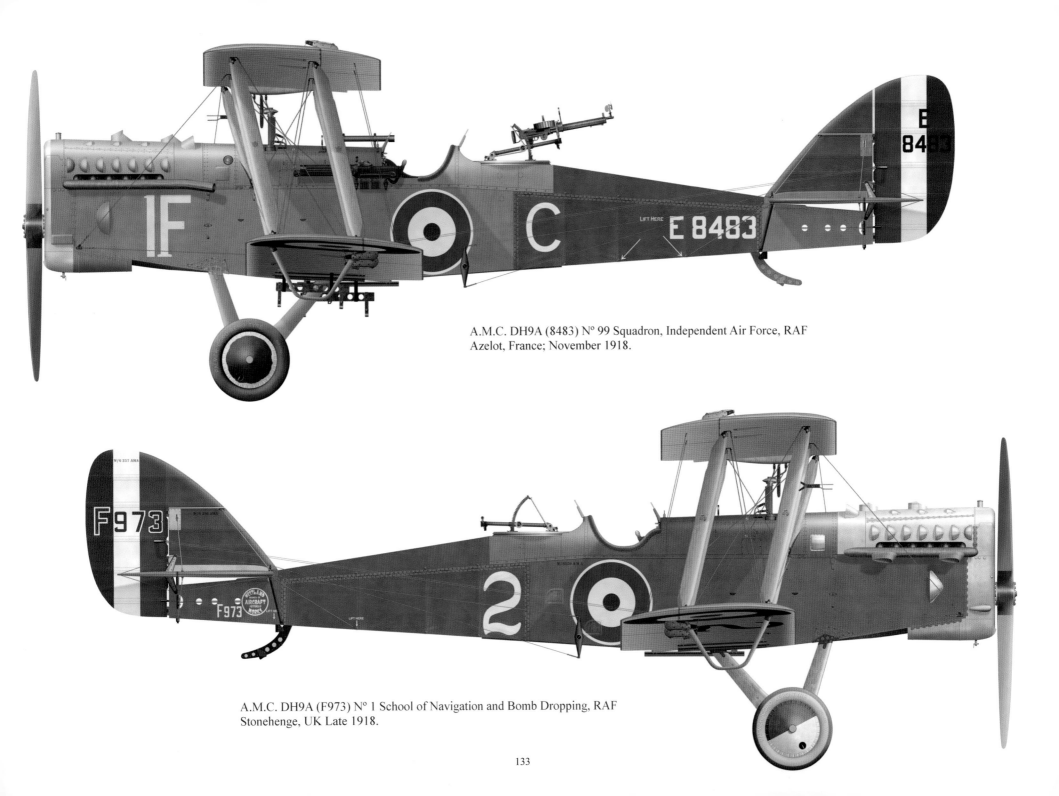

A.M.C. DH9A (8483) Nº 99 Squadron, Independent Air Force, RAF
Azelot, France; November 1918.

A.M.C. DH9A (F973) Nº 1 School of Navigation and Bomb Dropping, RAF
Stonehenge, UK Late 1918.